Breath

Breath & Spirit

REBIRTHING AS
A HEALING TECHNIQUE

Gunnel Minett

Aquarian/Thorsons
An Imprint of HarperCollinsPublishers

The Aquarian Press
An Imprint of HarperCollins*Publishers*
77–85 Fulham Palace Road,
Hammersmith, London W6 8JB
1160 Battery Street
San Francisco, California 94111-1213

Published by The Aquarian Press 1994
10 9 8 7 6 5 4 3 2 1
1 3 5 7 9 10 8 6 4 2

A catalogue record for this book
is available from the British Library

ISBN 1 85538 353 5

Phototypeset by Harper Phototypesetters Limited,
Northampton, England
Printed and bound in Great Britain by
Mackays of Chatham PLC, Chatham, Kent

Contents

The purpose of this book is not to teach you how to improve yourself, but to show you how great you already are.

Breath and Spirit by Gunnel Minett is a refreshing addition to the literature of Rebirthing. It is a gold mine of information and broad in its scope. It should be invaluable in academic circles and therapeutic circles as well as to Rebirthers and everyone who, as I, learned Rebirthing as a self-improvement skill. I enjoyed reading it myself because of the worldwide philosophical scope.

Rebirthing has always had two main aims for me. One is to learn to breathe energy as well as air. This is a specific, if intuitive skill that most people can learn in about ten Rebirthing sessions, each lasting one to two hours. It is a valuable skill that students can practise every day to refresh themselves and as a self-improvement and self-healing tool. It is a spiritual as well as a physiological skill that immensely contributes to our well-being emotionally as well as spiritually and physically.

The other aim is to unravel the birth-death cycle. This goal of total mastery of mind and body is beyond the stated goals of education, therapy, politics and most philosophy. Perhaps our theory and goals in these fields are too superficial.

I have long thought that our academic theory is still in the dark ages. The interest and mentality of the masses are way ahead of the formal academic world. Perhaps religious philosophy as well as scientific snobbery are the great barriers of human evolution.

My work and the minds and lives of many people will be enriched by this book.

Truth, simplicity and love

Leonard Orr
Founder of Rebirthing

Preface

The visible is not the only truth,
nor is it the whole truth;
the invisible must be penetrated
with the aid of the visible.

Marc Chagall

Simplex sigillum verum
(Simplicity is a sign of truth)
Herman Boerhaave, 1668-1738

The two quotes above, one by a great artist, the other by a great physician from the 17th Century (Boerhaave was a professor at the medical faculty of Lyden University, Holland, and one of the founders of the present scientific school of medicine) symbolizes the admirably whole and holistic view of human beings and life put forward in this book. In it, Gunnel Minett expresses a vision, striking in its simplicity and truth, of the potential which the healing power of conscious breathing promises for all of us.

The book fills a significant gap in today's medical and psychological literature and opens totally new perspectives, both for professionals and for interested lay people. It adopts the inter-disciplinary approach, characteristic of the New Age movement, at its best. It can serve as a model for a genuinely psychosomatic understanding of the life of an individual, in its indivisible continuity and totality.

Our medical and psychological philosophy is still deeply rooted in Cartesian dualism (Descartes, 1596-1760), which insists on a separation between body and soul, and between physical and psychological functions. Gunnel Minett demonstrates, with great clarity, the

x

spuriousness of these divisions. Life is a totality, an indivisible continuity, where all functions and processes, the so-called 'psychological' and the 'physical' represents a great complex pattern of mutual dependence and interdevelopment. New fields of medical research, such as biochemistry, endocrinology, immunology, etc, clearly reflect this new view of human life. New scientific theories and, above all, a new language are needed to link together this new thinking with the old terminology. This semantic situation is here pointed out by Gunnel Minett. Without doubt, semantic confusion still reigns in current scientific discourse, both in medicine and in psychology. Gunnel Minett's book is a considerable contribution towards greater clarity.

The book not only demonstrates the unity between body and soul, but also brings together other categories; theory and praxis, art and science, the subjective and objective reality, the prenatal and perinatal. The book is also a major contribution in the field of preventive medical theory. Health is more than absence of illness. I have earlier written that health is 'a dynamic movement on the creative road towards self-fulfillment' (1974). Gunnel Minett shows in her book what a contribution Rebirthing can make on this road.

Gunnel Minett's book, both in its theoretical and practical sections, provides a positive, creative and optimistic view of life: ' . . . be open to all possibilities, let no limiting thoughts stand in the way of personal development'.

I read the book with admiration and joy. It is my conviction that it will help all types of professional (therapists, doctors, psychologists, nurses) to a better understanding of their patients and enable patients to form a better understanding of themselves. It will encourage both groups to strive for better health, insight and quality of life.

Professor Peter G. Fedor-Freybergh, MD, PhD
December 1989

(Professor Fedor-Freybergh is an obstetrician and gynaecologist with a private clinic in Stockholm, Sweden. He is also a Professor of Psychoneuroendocrinology at the University of Salzburg, Austria, and has been the President of the International Society for Prenatal and Perinatal Psychology and Medicine (ISPP) since 1983.)

Introduction

This is not a conventional 'do-it-yourself' book about a psycho-therapeutic relaxation or meditation technique, nor is it simply a guide to a spiritual path. Birthing does not fall neatly into any of these categories. If Rebirthing was only a modern, Western, psycho-therapeutic technique and nothing else, this book would have had a conventional 'therapy book' approach, with case-studies and detailed descriptions of patients' 'recovery-processes'.

There are several reasons why I have chosen a different approach. First, the psychotherapeutic approach to Rebirthing has so far been the main aspect of the technique to be covered by the literature. This is the aspect that has provided a lot of interesting and exciting new insights about the human psyche. It was also the dominant aspect of the technique when it was first discovered and developed. Over the years, however, the technique has grown into more than just a psychotherapeutic tool. Along with this development, different schools and different approaches to Rebirthing have emerged. Some therapists have developed a more interventionist approach, where they combine the breathing with various other psychotherapeutic techniques. Other schools focus on the experience of the present moment, rather than the past, etc. As the title indicates, there is a close link between breath and spirit. This link has been experienced by many, in a personal and often very powerful way, during Rebirthing, and led to a broader and more complex understanding of the technique. This means that the description of the Rebirthing technique may vary between the different schools.

My position is that Rebirthing, in addition to being a very effective psychotherapeutic tool, also has a far wider and deeper cultural and historical significance, and it is this which my book explains and explores. This broader view is shared by the mainstream of the Rebirthing movement worldwide, including Leonard Orr, founder of Rebirthing, who states that, 'Rebirthing is not a therapy, but is self-improvement – it is an American form of "prana yoga".'

The British Rebirth Society (BRS) states in their information sheet that Rebirthing is a 'life-enhancement tool which is complementary to all other self-development and healing techniques: from meditation and mind-control to acupuncture and massage. Rebirthing has also been called "the science of enjoying all of your life".' Given the view that Rebirthing is a modern form of prana yoga, I found very soon that, in order to give a full picture of Rebirthing, I had to put it into a cultural and historical, as well as a psychological and medical context. The book is therefore an attempt to provide a broad, philosophical framework, within which the technique can be related and understood. The book is more concerned with explanations of *how the technique works* rather than just providing examples of its effects. Since this subject is, as yet, very little understood by Western science and medicine, I found it necessary to include what can be called 'spiritual explanations' of the technique from Eastern philosophies.

Another important reason for adopting this approach was that I had heard many people asking for a more overall explanation of Rebirthing – for example, the physical, mental, medical, philosophical implications. Rebirthing has developed almost entirely from subjective experience. There has, consequently, been a need for some form of conceptual framework to which these experiences can be related. The use of Eastern concepts, however, required a systematic, pedagogic and demystifying approach, because an adequate knowledge of such things as prana, chakras, kundalini, yin yang, reincarnation cannot be assumed among the public likely to be interested in Rebirthing. A lack of knowledge concerning these concepts sometimes leads to confusion and misunderstandings about the Rebirthing process.

I also think it would be gravely misleading to write a book about a breathing technique without reference to the fact that the modern Western view of breathing as simply satisfying the body's requirement for oxygen is culturally and historically anomalous: throughout history, in all cultures apart from that of modern industrial society, breathing has played an essential role in mystical and spiritual experiences. Reference to this is essentially important since so many people who practise Rebirthing have spontaneous and powerful spiritual experiences. The inability of Western medical and psychological professionals to adequately explain these experiences can lead to unnecessary confusion and distress.

This approach, however, required an attempt to cover a vast area of ideas and concepts. In order to keep the book to a reasonable size, I have been forced to deal with many topics in far too superficial a manner. The alternative was to exclude them altogether. Rather than do this, I have very briefly presented certain topics and tried to direct the interest to other sources, where they can more extensively be explored.

The book is divided into four parts. The first part, The Power of Breathing, describes how the Rebirthing technique is done and how conscious breathing is different from ordinary breathing. This part also includes some Eastern descriptions of conscious breathing and its various effects on the body and psyche.

The second part, The Physiology of Breathing, deals with how we breathe and what happens when we change our breathing pattern. It includes an Eastern version of human physiology. This differs from the Western since it is based on a subjective, rather than an objective experience of the body. This part also describes the healing power of breathing and how it has, historically, been used for medical purposes.

The third part, The Psychology of Breathing, describes how conscious breathing has always been used as a cleansing tool for the psyche. There are both old and new explanations for how this works. The section also contains a short account of other, modern techniques that focus on conscious breathing and some of the additional mental techniques that are often used in combination with Rebirthing.

The final part, The Spirituality of Breathing, gives an account of the original objective of conscious breathing - to serve as an aid to the attainment of higher levels of consciousness. Most people today who come into contact with Rebirthing know little or nothing about the ancient Eastern world views or Western spiritual matters. If they come to sessions, however, they often have experiences which lead them spontaneously into these areas. Because of this connection, this section aims to give a very brief overview of these matters.

I would like to finish by expressing my thanks to all who have helped me to get the book together. There are too many to name them all, but I am sure that they will all feel my gratitude anyway. I will, however, single out a few people. First of all, Shri Haidakhan Baba, whose energy is the source of my inspiration. Secondly, Leonard Orr, who has given me his support and has always been able to find time to read and discuss my manuscript and to provide useful comments despite his sometimes tight time schedule. I would also like to give my special thanks to Christina Davies who was kind enough to spend her whole Christmas holiday doing the rough editing of the manuscript. Last but certainly not least, I would like to thank my husband, Steve, for his tremendous patience, support and hard work throughout the whole production, but especially with the final editing of the finished book. And of course my son Michael, who provides an endless source of opportunities for me to learn about love, openness and a positive outlook on life.

Phuro! - Be inspired!
Om Shanti! - God's peace!
Gunnel Minett
January 1993

Rebirthing as a Healing Technique

I went to my first Rebirthing session without really knowing what to expect, since I knew nothing about the technique at all. I went to the session, basically because my boyfriend recommended me to see someone as I was feeling slightly depressed. I'd imagined I'd talk about myself and my problems and, probably, get some comforting and positive feedback.

The session turned out to be nothing of the kind: after a short introduction, I was asked to describe how I felt at that very moment; was I angry, sad, afraid or happy, etc.? I was encouraged to release these feelings during the session, without worrying about what they meant. Otherwise, I was simply given instructions on how to breathe during the session: 'Take a few deep breaths, then start breathing a little faster than normal'. As I tried to adopt this pattern of breathing, the instructions became more precise for each breath. I had no idea why I should breathe in this way. I had never previously given much thought to my breathing. It had never occurred to me that I could consciously select various different ways to breathe.

Despite this mental darkness, I soon fell into the 'correct' breathing pattern; something started happening to my body. My arms and legs contracted and became stiff. My face felt hard and bizarre. There was a tingling, 'pins and needles' sensation all over my body. I began to feel afraid and alone. Not because of what was happening during the session, but simply the emergence of a vague feeling of fear, which was spreading like a creeping chill over my body. I began to cry. Instead of being comforted or told to stop, I was instructed to continue to take long deep breaths and to avoid giving in to the crying. I complied and the urge to cry, centred around a lump in my throat, dissolved, as if in a series of waves which spread over the rest of my body, like ripples on a water surface. In their wake, I felt an enormous sense of relaxation and calm.

After the session I was not at all clear as to what had happened, but I felt different, more light-hearted. It was not the big change I had vaguely hoped for, and it was totally different from what I had expected. Yet I was rather pleased. In fact, I went back after a while ready to try again. Fifteen years later, I am still not totally clear about how the conscious breathing process 'works' (if that is the right word). All I can report is that the experiences it produces meant – and still mean – enough to me to want to continue with it on a regular basis.

Rebirthing is, for me, far more than a relaxation technique. Experiences during sessions have led me to transform my world view and approach to life. The power of these fantastic psychic journeys has driven me to seek some explanation. The search has lead me in many directions: into psychology, biology, history, modern physics and religion. When I got to the ancient Eastern scriptures, I started to feel that I was on to something. This lead eventually took me to India to find out more about the mysterious yogis, who seem to live under a different set of natural laws than ordinary human beings.

What I experienced in India convinced me that we are poised at the edge of a new era, when an understanding of full human potential will become universally accessible. What has been known to a few, throughout history, will probably soon be recognized by Western science. In so many areas, throughout modern science, current research is pointing to the need for a total paradigm shift. Much of what traditional psychology refers to as mental disorder or illness is seen from a new perspective by modern psychotherapy. Modern physics, which has been a pioneer of the new world view, has clearly shown that conventional Western models of reality are useful only over a very narrow range of experience. In quantum physics the same phenomenon can be either a particle or a wave – there is more than one approach. Modern psychology is learning that the biological and mental approaches to human behaviour and experience do not rule each other out; they simply adopt different perspectives to examine the same phenomenon. What can be seen as behavioural patterns can also be described in terms of chemical fluctuations in the body. They are still describing the same thing. The point is to look at the whole picture, to have an holistic approach.

Ancient Eastern scripture corresponds more closely to the latest findings of modern science than does the Newtonian–Cartesian world view. The circle of religion and science is about to be closed. Mystical explanations will no longer be esoteric. They'll become generally comprehensible and scientifically established.

Just as in the new physics, my personal search led me to the conclusion that every phenomenon in our lives can be simply described as energy, in some form: everything is alive. We are all parts of the same entity. We influence the world through our way of thinking and we are influenced in our way of thinking by the world around us. This has given me a more positive approach to life. There are no limits to experience other than those of our own creation. Don't argue for your limitations, unless you want to keep them. Aim at the stars and you will reach the treetops. If the world seems wrong, it may be that we can't see the whole picture or are constructing distorting limits to our perception of reality. We should try to be open to all possibilities and not let limiting thoughts stand in the way of our personal development. To many people, all this might appear obvious. I, however, had to have a number of breathing sessions before I could establish contact with that side of me which intuitively knew all this.

My intention with this book is to help to make available a marvellously efficient and powerful tool for psychological and spiritual growth which we all possess - by simply realizing the full potential of our own breathing apparatus. I've tried to do so by describing all aspects of conscious breathing (or, as it is more commonly known, Rebirthing): how it can help us to heal our bodies and minds, restore our full capacities, produce better physical performance and better access to our inner source of wisdom. In short, this simple, natural tool can restore our health and teach us to live in harmony with ourselves.

By focusing on the Rebirthing technique I do not imply any disparagement of other breathing techniques. However effective Rebirthing is, it is still a technique that has been developed over a very short period of time, compared with the ancient Eastern techniques. I am convinced that with a combination of modern research and ancient wisdom, conscious breathing can be developed into a very fine and precise tool to release and develop our inner resources. It is this ultimate, and as yet non-existent, breathing technique which is the real subject of this book.

Consequently, Rebirthing has to be placed in its historical context. A full account of the technique also requires an examination of what we know about the role of breathing in the body, both from the point of view of modern medical research and from ancient wisdom. As yet, there have been few specific scientific studies of conscious breathing. Hopefully there will be more in the near future. Despite this, a great deal is known about its effects from the records of subjective experiences. Some of these date back as far as human history. Others come from the observations of modern psychotherapy.

Throughout the book I relate personal experiences in order to illustrate the technique. The main reason for this is that, while a lot can be learnt about conscious breathing from historical, cultural, psychological and medical points of view, it is ultimately something intensely subjective, which just has to be experienced.

Leonard Orr, the main creator of Rebirthing, once told me about his amazement when he first started working with the technique. He was fascinated that he could actually get people to come and see him, lie down on his couch and let him listen to them breathing for about an hour, and happily pay him for doing next to nothing with them. He could not explain the technique to them, or tell them what went on, but it did not seem to matter. Although these people had very different experiences, they all agreed that something positive had happened to them and gladly came back for new sessions.

What is Rebirthing? How can something so simple have such an effect? Every living person breathes constantly. How can it make such a difference to breathe in a slightly different way? It is difficult to get a complete picture of what Rebirthing is about just by reading about it. The most important part is the personal experience. To those interested in what I describe, I would like to say: find a good Rebirther, try it and learn all about it. The experience of it exceeds anything that can be said about it. I do not say that Rebirthing is the only way to attain this kind of experience; far from it. What is most important is to find a key, wherever it may be, to our own inner wisdom and resources.

There is a well-known story about Buddha. A monk threatened to abandon his religious life if Buddha could not tell him whether a saint existed after death or not. The Buddha replied:

It is as if a man, wounded by a poisoned arrow, should say to the attending surgeon: 'I will not let this arrow be removed until I have learned the caste of the man who shot me. I have to know how tall he is, what family he comes from, where they live, what kind of wood his bow is made from, what fletcher made his arrows . . . His questions have nothing to do with getting the arrow out, and he would die before they were answered. Similarly, I do not teach whether the world is eternal or not eternal; whether it is finite or infinite; whether the soul and the body are the same or different . . . I teach how to remove the arrow.'

We live in a time of change. Everyone today is aware of the threats to our future generated by our own life style. It is not knowledge about how to change the world which is required, but rather the insight that we already have enough wisdom inside us to create a harmonious world. This change must start from within – from personal experience. Only insight can bring together the knowledge gathered patiently over centuries, with a total vision, and give us the courage to solve our problems.

9

Part 1

THE POWER OF BREATHING

1

Breathing and
Exceptional Performance

And the Lord God formed man
of the dust of the ground
and breathed into his nostrils
the breath of life;
and man became a living soul.

Genesis 2:7

In all cultures and throughout history breathing has been regarded as the most vital of human bodily functions. It was the cessation of breathing which determined the moment of death. Modern medicine has only recently, and amid great controversy, attempted to alter this ancient tenet of wisdom. A human lifetime is measured from the first to the last breath. Over and above this acknowledged biological supremacy, breathing has also been, fairly universally, seen as an important tool for physical, psychological and spiritual development.

With the possible exception of the modern Western world, breathing has always been seen as more than a simple, instinctive reflex to satisfy the body's need for oxygen. For millennia it has been understood that consciously controlled breathing can be used as a technique for enhancing mental and physical powers. Control of the breath has been applied to heal wounds and cure diseases; to prolong life and in order to achieve altered states of consciousness. Special, and specific, breathing techniques have been evolved to transcend the limits of our physical and mental abilities which we experience in every day life.

Breath, and the act of breathing, also has a spiritual dimension. Breath and spirituality are, in fact, indissolubly bound up with each other. One reason why breathing has lost its sacred standing in our modern Western cultures is that, until recently, our scientific world view had jettisoned spirituality entirely. The nineteenth-century ideology of Scientific Materialism which led to this rejection of spirituality came, in the West, to be incorporated into popular common thinking. Whereas, when seen in a broader cultural and historical context, it is really a rather peculiar view of reality – bizarre and alien when compared with the multitude of other conceptions of the nature of the world as devised by humankind throughout its history.

The Western 'Scientific' world view evolved over the last 300 years under the predominating influences of Descartes, Newton and Darwin. They created an objective, mental model of our world composed entirely of dead matter. This set of concepts has effectively diverted modern Westerners from the spiritual dimension of life; mental experience has become dominated by materialistic, logico-rational modes of thought. The ancient Eastern philosophies have, however, maintained their integrity, despite over a century of aggressive global expansion by the reductive 'modern' world view. While the latter takes matter as its point of departure for its account of the world, the Eastern traditions start with the psyche and spiritual experience as the fundamental realities. They see the unity between all living things in the universe and mankind's unity with the totality of existence.

Until very recently these two apparently irreconcilable world views were seen as simply antagonistic. The average Westerner tended to assume that the 'modern scientific' conception of reality would gradually supersede the ancient superstitions of the East. This complacent assumption has now been completely turned upside down. *And* this most unholy jolt has come from within the most sacred sanctum of Western scientific thinking – the discipline of physics. As the full implications of quantum mechanics and relativity theory have been unravelled during this century, physics has taken leave of its moorings in popular common sense. Whilst thrashing around for a new harbour on this sea of apparently total chaos, many leading theoretical physicists have sought an intellectual haven in the East. Its ancient accounts of the fundamental nature of reality provide a context for their findings which is simply more relevant than the Scientific Materialism in which they were brought up to believe.

Once the complacent shell of an assumed intellectual superiority had been cracked, the many thousand-year-old Eastern ways of seeing the world began to be re-evaluated in earnest. These world views could no longer be dismissed as simply ancient superstitions, since they seemed to offer a more accurate picture of scientifically revealed reality. What was required was a widening of the Western view to accommodate them, rather than the other way around. In certain cases today research hypotheses are being extracted from ancient Indian and Chinese texts. The circle of myth, religion and science is beginning to close again – despite continuing resistance from many institutional researchers.

Western medicine has also begun to take an interest in, for example, acupuncture and other Eastern medical techniques. Their effects are being taken seriously but are extremely difficult to explain because they arise from a completely different way of explaining the body's functioning. For this and other reasons, it is beginning to be accepted that the limitations we have set for human mental and physical abilities are far too narrow. Modern research has begun to investigate Indian yogis and has established that they can manipulate their bodily functions by willpower in a way that was formerly regarded as supernatural.

Much of this Western medical interest in Eastern traditions has been stimulated by the modern problem of stress. This phenomenon seems to be inextricably linked with industrialism and modern styles of life, and has spread with them all over the globe. It is now fairly generally accepted that the drug-based therapies of conventional Western medicine cannot provide a long-term solution to the problems of stress and may, in fact, exacerbate them. The problem of stress is forcing Western medicine to accept the reality of mind-body unity. What is really required to deal with this characteristic modern syndrome, are methods for re-establishing the natural harmony between body, mind and spirit.

During the last few decades a large number of different relaxation and meditation techniques aimed at achieving just this have been introduced in the West. Most of them owe a great deal to Eastern traditions and involve physical exercises, in which conscious control of the breath plays a prominent role. This may be just the beginning of a vast social trend that will completely transform the way we allocate human resources. Russell (1984) points out that agriculture was the major economic occupation on the planet in 1900. As the century progressed industry expanded rapidly. In the West, at the beginning of the 1970s, information and communication became the largest areas of economic activity. He suggests that, by the year 2000, the economy will be dominated by occupations concerned with exploring and developing the psychic potential of human beings.

The conscious control of breath may play a central role in this new human task. We still have a lot to learn about the latent human resources and energy which breathing techniques can release. The knowledge which we do have has been accumulated over several thousand years, mainly through introspective research and meditation. Only the most primitive technology was available to assist in this research process. Modern technology enables us to measure, for example, the minute changes in body chemistry which occur during meditation and other altered states of consciousness. It can, therefore, be confidently expected that even greater progress can now be made in this field. Learning to breathe in an optimal way may prove to be the key to unleashing the vast but virtually untouched treasure house of potential which we all possess:

> It is frequently stated that we use only 10 per cent of our full mental potential. This, it now appears, is rather an overestimate. We probably do not use even 1 per cent - more likely 0.1 per cent or less. The apparent limits of the human brain are only the limits of the uses to which we put it, and the limits of what we believe is possible.
>
> *Russell, The Brain Book, 1984*

It has long been known that, in certain extreme situations, people can produce 'hyper-performance' behaviours, way above the limits of what they themselves, or any other observer, could reasonably have expected of them. Mothers lift cars with their bare hands to save their children, people buried alive survive for incredible periods without food and water, and in emergencies people find themselves able to receive telepathic signals from across the globe, especially when others they are emotionally close to are in danger. This list could be greatly extended. The evidence for such phenomena is very convincing. It's only recently, however, that hyper-performance phenomena have begun to be seriously researched, usually in an effort to enhance athletic performance. Common factors associated with hyper-performance are emergency situations involving extremely strong emotional reactions coupled with a tremendous motivation on the part of the hyper-performer to help themselves or others.

This psychic element is now accepted in sports training. Peak performance cannot be attained simply by mechanically training the body. The mind too must be brought into play. This has always been recognized to a certain extent, but now the psychic element in athletic training is taking systematic and explicit forms. For example, muscle development is being advanced through mental visualization of manoeuvres: the results are claimed to be better than those achieved with conventional physical training.

Many other efforts are being made to try to map the psyche's influence on the body. The main objective is to identify those factors which were crucial on the occasions when outstanding performance has been demonstrated. One of the most famous examples of peak sports performance in recent years was the truly exceptional world record in the long jump set at the Mexico Olympics in 1968 by the American Bob Beamon, when he added an incredible 21.5 inches to the previous record. Ernst Jokl, Professor of Neurology at the University of Kentucky, described it as 'the greatest single feat in the recorded history of athletics' and as 'entirely inexplicable'. Beamon's own description of what happened is not very informative: 'I was frightened, man. I figured the pressure was on me. *I was between time and space*'. (Watson, 1987)

This last statement is rather mysterious and does imply an altered state of consciousness. A significant factor here may be the fact that this Olympics was held at a high altitude. In the Eastern traditions, it is known that high altitude can have a direct effect on the mind-body system. It is believed that the different quality of the air at high altitudes can affect the parts of the brain which control consciousness and especially the supply of energy to the muscles. In the various disciplines of yoga the effects of high altitude have long been known. Special breathing exercises, practised at high altitude retreats in the Himalayan mountains, have long been prescribed as a swift and effective method for changing the level of consciousness.

Recent research has also focused on the relationship between the two sides of the brain and its influence on human peak performance. Current theory suggests that highly successful individuals, especially those who are eventually labelled as geniuses, have an exceptional ability to integrate the two sides of their brains. They have unusually easy access to the intuitive right side of the brain – but they are not simply day-dreamers and fantasists: their genius consists of an ability to apply the right side's torrid outpourings to the disciplined, ordering activity of the logical, rational left side. Albert Einstein is one of the best-known examples in modern times. His theories, despite the mathematical rigour of their final form, had their origin in dreams and images: the theory of relativity was conceived one summer day as Einstein lay on a grassy slope and allowed his thoughts to run free. Leonardo da Vinci was another such 'brain-balanced' genius. He used his outstanding artistic ability in the entire range of his incredibly varied activities, but combined it always with strict, logical thought. The result is a matter of historical record – priceless masterpieces of fine art plus technical designs so advanced that their originality can only now, with our present level of technology, be fully appreciated.

2

The Rebirthing Technique

Breath is the key to the mystery of life, to that of the body as well as to that of the spirit.

Lama Anagarika Govinda

Breathing is the interaction between our inner selves and the surrounding atmosphere. When we breathe we absorb, in addition to physical substances, the surrounding reality into our inner system. It is essential, therefore, both for physical and psychological well-being, that our breathing is optimal. On the purely physical level, for example, the manner in which we breathe is highly significant for the condition of our inner organs, dependent as they are on oxygen from the blood. But as we shall see, breathing also affects the mental and spiritual aspects of ourselves.

Rebirthing, or conscious breathing, is the name of a particular breathing technique. Very briefly, it can be described as a relaxed, connected and total way of breathing, similar to the way most people breathe during deep sleep. This breathing pattern triggers a natural process of cleansing and purifying in both the body and the psyche. The combination of deep relaxation, openness of the body and mind, and increased oxygen intake, tends to dissolve everything that stands in the way of the body's natural circulation.

The process has been found to be a very precise key to the body's natural healing resources. Once the process is initiated, the body seems to know exactly how to cleanse and revitalize itself. Although it is a purely physical exercise, the process does not just affect the body but also has a direct effect on the psyche. The expansion of the body's circulation systems, through relaxation and the increased speed

19

of circulation, facilitates the release of chemicals into the bloodstream. This has a cleansing effect on both the body and the psyche. The chemicals released into the system can, when they reach the brain, be perceived and interpreted as memories and previous experiences.

Wilder Penfield (1976) showed that it was possible to trigger photographic memories by touching various areas of the brain with an electrode during brain surgery. The Rebirthing breathing technique has been found to be an equally powerful tool for releasing old memories. The fact that the process is initiated by physical activity, not mental – through increased openness, relaxation and circulation – makes it possible to release memories from the very earliest stages of life. Before the brain was fully developed memories were recorded and stored in various parts of the body, as bodily sensations. It is not possible to reach this type of memory through the mind. These early memories have not left a sufficient imprint in the brain, only in the area of the body which was involved in the original experience. The cleansing effect on the body is often felt as an increase in energy. It can also generate a mental sharpening that brings the body to a higher level of functioning both physically and psychologically.

Of all the modern breathing techniques available today, Rebirthing is the only one that focuses entirely on breath as the tool for cleansing, revitalizing and purifying the body. In many schools of modern psychotherapy, breath is used as a tool to get in touch with subconscious thoughts and feelings. They are then dealt with through some form of mental and emotional catharsis. In Rebirthing, however, the focus is entirely on the breath. Maintaining a relaxed, open pattern of breathing is the key to our inner selves. The underlying assumption is that every thought and emotion is also a form of energy and can be expressed as such – through the breath. This makes the technique especially relevant, because an absolutely essential aspect of healing the body and mind involves changing the way we breathe.

LIFE ENERGY

Rebirthing can also be described, like ancient breathing techniques, as a method of activating the 'life energy' by opening up the body's full breathing capacity. Life energy is a concept which has a central significance in Eastern cultures but is more or less unknown in the West. The Eastern concept is described at greater length in later chapters. Here, life energy can simply be understood as the driving force for the body and the psyche. Activating it leads to a sense of harmonious openness and an ability to experience and use the body and the psyche in a completely unrestricted way.

We in the western world have a long tradition of physical and mental health care, but we totally lack any tradition of working with pure life energy. It is a part of the picture that has been totally lost for us. Working with the direct life energy is like giving people a new tool. In today's world many people are so depressed that they completely lack the energy to even begin to deal with their problems. They need more life energy in order to be able to deal with their situation and to receive inspiration to struggle for a change. They also need more life in the body in order to be able to feel and experience themselves. It can be said that breathing is our most unused natural resource. Breathing provides the greatest potential for positive changes.

From an interview with Bo Wahlström, co-founder and head teacher at the Swedish Rebirther Training Centre, February 1989

The method of breathing in Rebirthing is designed to open up the body's natural energy streams; to stimulate their circulation so that the energy of the body can flow unhindered. This enhancement of the body's energy circulation provides optimal conditions for the body and the psyche to unfold their inherent abilities. Among these are powerful natural drives for physical and psychological healing. Rebirthing can stimulate a quicker renewal of cells, facilitating the body's renewal and vitalization.

The stimulation, however, is achieved through relaxation. The relaxation enables blocked memories to be released (see Chapter 8). These memory blocks are associated with experiences which, for some reason, have not been worked through and integrated physically and mentally; they have been simply pushed down into the unconscious. These blockages can hinder or actively work against our conscious intentions. By resolving and releasing them, a higher level of consciousness can be attained: psychic energy can be more effectively focused on present, consciously-chosen tasks, leading to an improved level of performance.

Rebirthing takes as its basic model the pattern to be found in the natural breathing of small children and people peacefully asleep. In other words, the breathing of a harmonic and totally relaxed person. (In actual Rebirthing sessions, the intensity of the breathing can be much higher than in everyday life.) In the modern world it is difficult to find adults who still have this basic, natural breathing pattern, with the exception of certain isolated groups of primitive people. Nearly all adults have, to a greater or lesser extent, constant muscular tension and energy blocks. Of all the body's functions, it is in breathing that these aberrations manifest themselves most. Their effects on breathing prevent the body functioning at its full capacity.

THE DEVELOPMENT OF THE TECHNIQUE

Although Rebirthing has clear links with ancient Eastern breathing techniques, it cannot simply be said to be a rediscovery of the old methods. Rebirthing was developed in America in the early 1970s, mainly by Leonard Orr. He evolved the technique purely by experimenting with various breathing patterns and studying their effects on the body and psyche. Despite this independent origin, the technique that has emerged has many similarities with the ancient techniques.

The development of Rebirthing can be described in the following way. Orr first noticed that changing the breathing produced dramatic and/or bizarre experiences. When explanations for these experiences were sought, the medical and psychological literature did not provide much guidance. There were no descriptions of variations in the breathing patterns, or observations of how breathing influenced the body and psyche. The only explanations that fully recognized the importance of various breathing patterns were found in the Eastern schools of yoga and Chi Gong, etc. Eastern knowledge has, therefore, come to form a theoretical foundation for the method.

Initially, Orr was not doing systematic psychological research. He describes his early work as simply a step in a more general search for 'methods of self-improvement'. To begin with, this search consisted mainly of Orr subjecting his own body to different types of external influence. He spent extremely long periods in the heat of a sauna and kept his body submersed in warm or cold water for several hours in order to see what effects this would have. He soon discovered that certain situations lead to strong emotional reactions. He recalled memories of traumatic situations, often related to birth. He also noted that these experiences lead to a spontaneous change in the breathing pattern. He therefore began to experiment with various ways of breathing, in an attempt to reproduce the rhythms he had observed. This led to even stronger reactions and more vivid memory experiences of his own birth and other traumatic events. Later on, he began to teach others how to obtain these experiences. He would sit with them and guide their breathing in order to reproduce the patterns he had discovered. He found that most people reacted as he had done, with the birth trauma as a common element in their experiences.

This recurrence of experiences relating to birth led to the method becoming known as Rebirthing, but it is also known by several other names, the most common of these being Conscious Breathing, Conscious Connected Breathing and Spiritual Breathing. In the beginning, Orr conducted all breathing exercises in warm water, thinking that the water was essential to the experience. Orr had his first 'spontaneous' rebirthing experiences submerged in very hot water (see pages 50–51). Participants lay submersed in water either floating on their backs or face down (in the latter case they breathed through a snorkel). As an alternative to the hot water sleeping bags were used.

23

People would lay in them for periods of up to fourteen hours, in order simulate the pre-natal environment. Sessions in these specially contrived conditions often led to intensely strong emotional reactions. The participant had to be removed from the special environment in order to finish off the session in a calmer setting. This development led successively to an abandonment of the contrived environments. 'Dry sessions', which lead to the same reactions but in calmer circumstances, became the standard practice.

Leonard Orr discovered that as an individual progressed through a series of breathing sessions, the strong emotional reactions would disappear if the person could interpret the implications of the traumatic experience they were reliving. This process later became known as integration (see Chapter 8). Integration generally led not only to the disappearance of the traumatic reaction, but also to a dissolution of the complex of behaviour patterns associated with it. Sometimes a memory might recur on several occasions and lead to many insights before it was finally dissolved. Only when the whole event had been re-experienced and interpreted would it disappear totally from the breathing sessions.

A Personal Experience

In America, at the end of a six-week intensive training course with Leonard Orr, I received the second of my private sessions with him. 'I want to show you how to discover your natural breathing rhythm', he said by way of introduction to the exercises. He carefully guided each breath I took. 'A little longer, a little deeper' he said in the beginning. But he was soon saying 'a little less, a little less', until I had almost stopped breathing altogether. My breathing was so slight as to be hardly noticeable. 'Pay attention now', he said. 'Remain completely still for a moment – there!', he observed, 'and there again. Did you notice the tiny, tiny breath that happened entirely by itself? That is your natural breathing. Become conscious of it and let it develop. That is what you should focus your attention on as we continue.'

THE OPTIMAL ENVIRONMENT

The ideal environment for a Rebirthing session should be completely calm and secure, without any external disturbances or stimuli. When disturbances do occur they often lead to associations which stimulate significant memories. (Outer stimuli should, therefore, be controlled, to avoid interruption and disturbance of inner processes.) Above all, it is important to create a sense of security, so that there is nothing in the outer environment which might hinder the re-experiencing of blocked memories.

Rebirthing is best practised lying on the back with the feet falling naturally apart and the hands at the sides with the palms upward. (This position in yoga is known as shavasana). It is important to lie on something comfortable, flat and not too soft, so that the body rests in a straight position, which is physically best for breathing. Changes of position are common during Rebirthing, so it is necessary to have enough space to be able to move around. Curling up into the fetal position is a very common reaction as a response to fear or during experiences connected with birth. It is also important not to feel cold. Reliving certain experiences can induce intense feelings of being cold, or even freezing, so it is very useful to have a blanket close by.

VARIOUS FORMS OF BREATHING SESSION

It is strongly recommended that one's first Rebirthing sessions should be conducted under the supervision of an experienced therapist. The first reactions to the technique can be intense, unfamiliar and sometimes rather frightening for someone who is new to this kind of exercise. The experience can therefore be overwhelming unless guidance is available from someone familiar with the process. An experienced Rebirthing therapist can give support and assist the novice breather to maintaining the correct breathing pattern (which is the best safeguard against negative reactions). When enough blocked material has been released, however, most people feel safe enough to do it alone or together with a friend who can give sufficient support. A common arrangement is to exchange sessions, taking turns to guide and to breathe. Since the technique can be done alone, it is a very useful tool during stressful periods. It can also be used to enhance performance on special occasions, as a relaxation method, or to provide extra energy.

Breathing sessions can also be conducted in hot or cold water. Hot water sessions are done in a heated pool or bath tub, large enough for three or more people to move around freely. The breather floats on the back with only the head above the water. Alternatively, the breather floats on the stomach, face down, with the whole body submerged, using a special 'double-type' snorkel that gives a sufficient supply of fresh air throughout the session. The temperature of the water should be between 38.0 and 38.9°C to simulate conditions in the womb. Sufficient physical support must be provided, so that the breather can relax and the whole session can be carried out in total safety. The therapist therefore has an assistant, who concentrates on holding the body afloat and giving the necessary support. This way the Rebirther can concentrate on supervising every breath, without having to be interrupted or distracted by safety concerns.

Water sessions can also be done in cold water, for example in unheated outdoor pools. The breathing rhythm should be established before entering the water. Immersion should be gradual, so that the connected breathing can be maintained despite the body's reaction to the cold water. If the body becomes tense, and relaxed breathing can no longer be maintained, the whole process should be restarted out of the water. Hot water tends to trigger memories from the womb and the first phase of birth. Cold water stimulates memories of temperature changes at birth and near death experiences.

It is important to emphasize here that Rebirthing sessions should always be conducted in a calm and totally safe environment, so that the breather can focus uninterruptedly on his/her inner self. This is even more important if the session is being conducted in water, which can amplify the physical and emotional reactions. **Under no circumstances should a water session be carried out without at least two people standing in the water to support the person breathing!**

It is essential that these rules are clearly stated in any reference to Rebirthing in water, and strictly adhered to in its practice. This is necessary, not only for the safety of all involved, but also to firmly dispel certain rumours concerning the dangers of Rebirthing in water. The origin of these rumours was a tragic accident which took place in Devon, in December 1991, during a group leadership training course. This course did *not*, however, include Rebirthing in the programme. Following this incident, several newspapers reported that a man had drowned during a water Rebirthing session. This, however, is completely untrue.

Since this reported accident seemed to contradict all my previous experiences of water Rebirthing, I was therefore anxious to get the full details in order to find out what had actually happened. I obtained the complete transcript of the Coroner's report on this case. Neither the Coroner nor the pathologist who conducted the autopsy, nor any of the thirteen witnesses who made sworn statements, mention the word 'Rebirthing' or anything connected with the technique. The report clearly states that the man died from accidental drowning while he was swimming underwater, alone, in the training centre's swimming pool during a leisure period before the actual training had started. His activity was totally self-initiated and had nothing to do with the conduct of the course (or with Rebirthing). He had, furthermore, been advised by the other participants not to swim alone. He nevertheless persisted and was found at the bottom of the pool, and did not respond to the efforts made to revive him.

Rebirthing can also be done in groups. Group sessions can be arranged either in pairs or in groups of three, or with several guides for a larger group of people lying side by side and breathing simultaneously. The guides walk around the group and concentrate on the person who most needs assistance at that time. Group sessions can use the group dynamic to provoke blocked memories. A person having difficulties expressing a feeling can often be helped by experiencing other people's emotional reactions to similar feelings. These can often be a mutual reinforcement which can serve as a powerful trigger for emotional expression.

Group sessions usually conclude with a group 'sharing', i.e. each participant is given a chance to describe his or her experiences during the session. These sharings are led by the therapists but all the participants are encouraged to comment and give feedback. The idea is that everyone should be their own therapist and find their own explanations and insights. The therapist's and the other participants' comments provide support for the understanding and integration process. Group sharing can also be a much longer-term process. For example, annual seminars or permanent support groups can be established, which meet regularly to share experiences of individual sessions and general personal development.

REBIRTHING AND ORDINARY BREATHING
- THE DIFFERENCES

There are three principal differences between the pattern of breathing in Rebirthing and ordinary breathing. First, Rebirthing is more rhythmic. The pattern of breathing should be made as rhythmic and even as possible. A visual analogy would be the rhythmic motion of waves effortlessly rolling in and out onto a beach. Secondly, Rebirthing requires an unbroken continuity of inhalation and exhalation: as soon as an inhalation is complete, the air should be allowed to begin to flow out again without the slightest pause between the different motions. This is one of the secrets of Rebirthing. The slightest pause between inhalation and exhalation is sufficient to restrict the natural flow of the breath, with negative consequences. Thirdly, the achievement of a tensionless exhalation: the air flowing out in the exhalation should be expelled exclusively by the weight of the chest falling. By completely relaxing the chest muscles, the chest simply sinks down during exhalation thus forcing out air from the lungs. No muscular exertion should be involved at all.

A Personal Experience

Having practised Rebirthing regularly for about a year, I undertook a session one autumn afternoon. We were in a large house in the countryside.

It was quite cold both indoors and out and the daylight had begun to disappear soon after I began my session. It was difficult to breathe and I was on the point of falling asleep several times. After a while I was advised to begin massaging a special point at the end of the little finger, just under the finger nail. This would enable me to stay awake.

This worked very well and my breathing became more connected. I began to become aware of the increasing darkness in the room and the cold which began to spread over my body. I asked for a blanket but this did not help very much. The cold was coming from inside. The experience was soon so strong that I felt myself totally numb and entered a state between sleep and consciousness. I began to 'dream'. (That is, I drifted off to a stage between sleep and wakefulness where I saw many dream pictures. At the same time I was awake enough to know that I was in the middle of a Rebirthing session.)

There were people standing around my bed. I had the feeling that the bed became larger and was surrounded by the wooden railings of a cot. I lay alone, without contact with the people around me. Suddenly, a grey man came up to me and stretched his arms down to lift me up. He exuded a strong sense of death and cold. I felt gripped by a rising tide of terror. I wanted to scream, to crawl away, to get the people around me to see that he was about to steal me away. I 'knew' that if he lifted me up and carried me away I would die, but nobody saw me, nobody heard my noiseless cries for help.

As so often in dreams, I awoke without experiencing the end. After the session, when I was considering what I had experienced, my first association was with the 'memory' of the time when I had whooping cough at the age of three months. There had been a point, I have been told, when it was life threatening for me. The grey man who was about to take me away from the bed was a symbol of death. The people who stood motionless around my bed were my powerless parents. The outer circumstances in the room during the session had probably set off the association with this period of illness. The images evoked were something between memories and dreams.

THE ENERGY CYCLE

Leonard Orr defines conscious breathing as 'breathing energy as well as air'. In order to achieve a successful Rebirthing session it's necessary to trigger a phenomenon known as 'the energy cycle'. The energy cycle will begin to operate when a pattern of intense, relaxed and connected breathing has been attained. This pattern should be effortless, despite being far more powerful and intense than normal breathing. All parts of the breathing apparatus are, at best, utilized and the entire body is energized. When the relaxation of the body, in combination with the increased breathing, has led to a sufficient opening of the body, the whole system will be directly affected by the breath. The breathing and relaxation will reach and penetrate every part of the body. The body starts 'to breathe energy as well as air'. This means that the body is starting to release inner, stored energy, while at the same time it is activated by the new energy brought in by the intensified breathing. This is a state referred to as 'inner breathing' in the yoga tradition (see pages 149-51). When this state is reached, the energy sweeps through the body and 'flushes out' all the previously stored energy. This energy has been stored in the form of organic chemicals or hormones which, when released, provoke memories. The energy cycle is the actual healing part of the Rebirthing process.

A necessary precondition is total relaxation, especially during exhalation. One way to achieve this is to increase the pace of breathing, while at the same time keeping complete continuity between the inhalation and the exhalation. In everyday life we control our breathing, for the most part, by making a pause between the inhalation and exhalation, by forcing out the breath during exhalation or by holding back the exhalation by slowly and carefully releasing the breath.

In the initial phase of a Rebirthing session, in order to attain a strong, relaxed rhythm, breathing should be consciously made more powerful and quicker than usual. Each breath should be about the same length as in normal breathing but with an increased capacity. This will fill the lungs to a greater extent than in normal breathing. Such a relaxed rhythm acts as a 'danger over' signal to the body's defence mechanisms (see Chapter 8). It normally requires only a short period, between one to thirty minutes of intense breathing, for the body's controls to feel safe enough to 'drop their guard' and open up the inner gate system. The breathing pattern then becomes more or less spontaneous.

During a session, breathing should be done either completely through the nose (both inhalation and exhalation) or completely through the mouth. It has been observed that this choice does, in fact, have significance: in most cases, breathing through the nose results in a more intellectual or spiritually-oriented insight into the experiences which emerge, while breathing through the mouth is more likely to lead to purely physical experiences. Nose-breathing is often said to have a more healing effect than mouth-breathing. It seems to be easier for the psyche to integrate and accept experiences that are linked with an intellectual or intuitive insight, than experiences on a purely physical level. It is common, and sometimes advisable, to switch from nose- to mouth-breathing, or vice versa, depending on the body's reactions during a session.

Most frequently, at the beginning of a session the person will be instructed to breathe high up in the chest. The upper chest is, for many people, where the blocking of respiration starts. In everyday life, it is the least utilized part of the breathing system and its activation is important for overcoming energy blocks. As soon as inhalation is complete, the air should be allowed to flow out again. This continuity is achieved by completely relaxing the muscles of the diaphragm. As the chest descends the volume of the lungs is reduced and the air is driven out by this motion. In certain cases this course of events can be directly influenced by adopting one of two alternative styles of breathing. (Conscious influence should only, however, be exercised over inhalation – exhalation should always be completely relaxed and undirected.) One style consists of taking very short and intensive breaths, the other of taking long and deep breaths. The short, intensive breath method leads to exhaustion of the muscles in the breathing organs and makes it more difficult to maintain control over breathing. This method can be used when it is necessary to break through an emotional block. The long, deep breathing method is of assistance when experiencing powerful emotional reactions which one might want to express in crying or screaming. It's possible to steer emotional reactions by breathing deeply and powerfully, in so far as the body's defence system will allow. It may also be desirable, however, on certain occasions, to let the feelings take over, without attempting to maintain the rhythm of breathing. At these times, whatever feelings emerge during the session are given free expression. When the peak of the emotional storm is over, rhythmic breathing should be resumed in order to complete the energy cycle. It is important to complete the energy cycle in every breathing session. In situations where the energy cycle has, for some reason, not been completed in the session, it is advisable to try to schedule a new session fairly soon afterwards. If the session is not completed the evoked memories tend to influence the psyche and can cause negative experiences later.

In addition to varying the pattern, the breathing effort can also be directed to different parts of the body: if the aim is to activate the upper part of the body, breathing should be done mainly in the upper part of the chest. If the concern of the session is with the lower parts of the body, then breaths should be taken predominantly in the lower parts of the chest and, to a certain extent, also in the abdomen. In addition, by concentrating attention on a particular part of the body and 'breathing into that area', memory experiences that are especially connected with it can be activated. Just before a session, pain, irritation, tension or some other form of disturbance, is often experienced in a localized part of the body, or in a particular bodily function. Such signs are often a clear indication that the memory experiences especially connected with these areas are ready to be worked through.

A Rebirthing session will normally last between one and three hours. What decides the duration of the session is the length of the energy cycle. When the rhythmic breathing has been attained the body will react by making the breathing more automatic and intense. This progression will reach a climax and then decline, successively, in order to gradually return to a normal, calm breathing rhythm. This course of events is completely spontaneous, without any conscious control: 'it was if someone took over and did my breathing for me', is a common reaction.

Sometimes breathing will stop completely, for several minutes, at the end of the energy cycle. This happens completely unconsciously and breathing resumes again automatically. There is no sense of unpleasantness associated with this experience. Most people in breathing sessions are completely unaware of the changes in their breathing patterns and most often describe experiences of a religious or transpersonal character. The course of events during a breathing session is not affected by whether a person is intellectually aware of the methods of Rebirthing or not. What influences and changes the pattern of breathing is simply the reactions which stored memories bring about.

The body reacts not only with automatic breathing during the energy cycle, but also with various sensations, such as bubbling and 'pins and needles'. These sensations are mainly quite pleasant. They may begin in one particular part of the body and then gradually spread to include the whole body. Sometimes this may be followed by experiences involving sound and light sensations, or simply by a general feeling of well-being. A feeling of stillness and total harmony is very often experienced.

When a complete energy cycle is being worked through a great deal of energy is released in the body. This is the origin of experiences of vibrations, tingling, etc. Tension is being released, since the main purpose of inner tension is to hold blocked energy under control. When the tensions are released they no longer block the body's energy flows. This results in an 'energy surplus', which most people experience after a session - a feeling of revitalization and abundant energy.

The energy release gives you a new body. You feel connected to your body in a wonderful way - sensually - abundant physical energy and a sense of safety and serenity spreads over you.

Ray, Orr, *Rebirthing in The New Age, 1977*

A Personal Experience

During my first Rebirthing session with Leonard Orr I was very nervous, simply because I was afraid of not doing it right. So when he began to guide me, in a very assured way, indicating the length and intensity of every breath, I was very concerned to do exactly as he said. As a result, we soon came to function as a single individual: Leonard could control my breathing just as he pleased. After a short period my body began to tingle. This was not a new experience, but I began to feel that I was losing control over what was happening.

My body began to curl up as if I was suffering from cramps, but there was no pain. My whole body was tingling more intensively than ever. Even my cheek bones and the roots of my hair were tingling and seemed to be curling up. My breathing became almost totally automatic and I needed only sporadic guidance. I completely lost any sense of space and time. The only thing I was conscious of was the tingling in my body and a vague image of someone observing what was happening.

After the session I was completely dizzy and had to hold on to the walls in order to get out of the room. It took several hours before I once again felt that I had both feet on the ground. But in the days immediately after the session I had a marvellous sense of lightness and felt very alert and filled with positive energy.

DIFFERENT TYPES OF BREATHING

Four general types of breathing can be identified in an average breathing session. They may all appear during one session, or they may vary between sessions depending on the special circumstances which predominate in each session:

Deep and Slow Breathing

This kind of breathing is often recommended at the beginning of a session, before switching to consciously connected and rhythmic breathing. This style of breathing aids the transition to a relaxed and meditative state of mind. It is also used at the end of a session, when the emotional reactions to the memories relived during the session are in the process of being integrated.

Short and Swift Breathing

This can be used in the next phase of the session, when sufficient relaxation has been achieved and attention has been directed inward. It is a preliminary to connected breathing. In order to get the body adjusted to more intense and relaxed breathing, this pattern has first to be imposed by conscious effort. After a while, when the body's systems start responding to this style of breathing, it 'takes over'. The body then regulates the breathing in a very effective and effortless manner. The short, swift style should also be adopted during the most intense phases of a session, when powerful emotional and physical reactions occur.

Swift and Deep Breathing

This is to be used mainly in situations where the body's defence mechanisms are triggered in an attempt to block certain memory experiences. This can lead to a numbing reaction and/or a sleep-like condition. To overcome this, it may even be necessary, on occasions, to breathe in a sitting or standing position, or even walking, in order to escape the numbness. It is especially memories from earliest childhood which may lead to this sort of reaction, because sleep is the only possible defence for an infant against too painful stimuli.

Fully Relaxed and Connected Breathing

During most of a Rebirthing session, breathing should be experienced as automatic and effortless. Each breath should be deep and all of the body's breathing apparatus should be in use. The breathing cycle should be continuous, with no pauses between inhalation and exhalation, and the breathing process should be completely relaxed.

This type of breathing should occur when the body has adjusted to the changed breathing pattern which is consciously initiated at the beginning of a session. It occurs when enough blocked energy has been released to enable the body to use its full capacity, without restrictions. This type of breathing is very often accompanied by tingling sensations throughout the body, when the newly-released energy begins to flow around the body. During the first Rebirthing sessions it may be difficult to attain this type of total breathing because there may be a lot of tension in the body, which first has to be worked through. But for the experienced breather this type of breathing can be maintained throughout most sessions for most of the time.

3

Conscious Breathing
in Traditional China

꧁

Rebirthing was developed in modern times by trial and error, as a method for psychological and spiritual development. As explained earlier, there is no real tradition of breathing exercises, nor explanations of their effects, in the Western culture. Having presented the Rebirthing technique in detail, we have to look further afield for explanations. Comparisons with similar techniques developed in other parts of the world, especially the East, provide the most fruitful source. Over thousands of years a great number of very precise breathing exercises have been developed and recorded, designed for medical or psychological purposes or to be used as a tool to expand consciousness for religious purposes.

We will start with the great cultural traditions of conscious breathing found in the Chinese tradition. As we shall see, there are many similarities between the various breathing patterns in the Chinese exercises and those recognized in Rebirthing. One Chi Gong exercise in particular, known as 'the Breathing of Love', seems to be exactly the same as the pattern of breathing which predominates in successful Rebirthing sessions.

The main breathing technique in the Chinese tradition is called Chi Gong. 'Chi' is the Chinese word for life energy. 'Gong' means exercise. The practice of Chi Gong is traditionally referred to as 'the method to eliminate illness and prolong life'. The Chinese do not recognize any necessary contradiction between the ancient body of knowledge about the human body and soul, which they have inherited, and modern scientific research, employing the most advanced technology.

This attitude is illustrated by the several scientific studies of various Chi Gong practices, which have been carried out over recent decades. Among other things, these have established that several natural, physical emissions from the body, such as infra-red radiation, static electricity and various particle radiations, are all affected in a measurable way by the practice of breathing according to Chi Gong methods. (Zang, 1985)

Over the centuries the Chinese have learnt to distinguish the most subtle nuances between various types of breathing. As a result, they have developed a range of highly sophisticated breathing techniques, each evolved for use in a particular area of life. (With the typical Chinese flair for lyrical expression, each technique is named after its intended effect.) The Chinese divide the effects of breathing into three categories: effects on the body, effects on the psyche, and effects on the spirit. The variables which produce these effects are variations in the speed of breathing, the depth of each breath, and the length of each breath.

Slow Breathing

The physical effect of slow breathing is to slow down the metabolism, heartbeat and blood circulation. Psychologically, it leads to a calmer, more peaceful state of mind, with clearer thoughts and a more objective understanding. It also increases our sensitivity towards others. On the spiritual level, it leads to broader perception, deeper insights and a wider contact with universal consciousness. Here are some examples of slow breathing techniques.

The Breathing of Unselfishness

This is so still and slow that a piece of rice paper in front of the face will not move. It is meant to calm down all bodily activities and to prepare for meditation. It is also used as a tool to recognize egocentric distortions in one's perception of the surrounding world.

The Breathing of Harmony
This pattern is slightly more powerful than the latter. It gives a peaceful and harmonic contact with the surrounding world and a greater awareness of it.

The Breathing of Self-Esteem
This is slightly faster than the previous ones. Its purpose is to enhance the harmony between the various bodily functions and give increased self-esteem.

The Breathing of Activity
Here each breath is long, deep and powerful, and taken through a slightly open mouth. Its purpose is to activate all physical, psychological and spiritual forces so that one can react to the surrounding world without losing objective perception. It is also used to release physical and psychological blockages and leads to general relaxation.

Quick Breathing

The effect of quick breathing on the body is to speed up the metabolism, heartbeat and blood circulation. Psychologically, it provides an unstable and more easily affected state of mind, leading to faster emotional changes. Spiritually, it generates subjective and egocentric values and perceptions of the world, with greater emphasis on details.

Shallow Breathing

Here the metabolism becomes less active and there is less integration between its various functions. On the psychological level, shallow breathing produces a tendency to worry, mental instability and dissatisfaction, often leading to fear. Spiritually, perception becomes superficial, with many distractions.

Deep Breathing

This causes the metabolism to become more active and more efficient and harmonic. Psychologically, it creates deep feelings of satisfaction, emotional stability and strong self-esteem. Spiritually, it leads to greater thoughtfulness, greater trust and openness and a more loving attitude. An example of deep breathing is:

The Breathing of Spirituality

This pattern is long, deep and powerful. Breath is taken through the mouth, while forming the words 'hi' (spirit, fire, sun) and 'fu' (wind, expansion). It activates the physical and psychological metabolism and brings the person into contact with his or her spirituality.

Long Breaths

At the bodily level, this produces greater coordination between the various functions of the metabolism. Activity in the organs and glands tends to become slower. Psychologically, long breaths create greater peacefulness and feelings of satisfaction, greater perseverance and a calmer temperament. Spiritually, they lead to deeper and more objective insights and understanding. Here are some examples of long breath forms.

The Breathing of Intelligence

This is done in the throat and the area around the root of the tongue. Its purpose is to develop physical and psychological concentration. It gives a clear perception and deep insight into present problems.

The Breathing of Tan-Den

This is deep and slow, with natural movements of the diaphragm, which is regarded in Chinese anatomy as the centre of the body and a storage point for energy. The purpose of this pattern is to provide physical energy and psychological stability. It gives a feeling of steady anchoring on earth and makes it easier to stay uninfluenced by the surrounding world.

The Breathing of Love

This is done in the upper part of the chest with a slow inhale and exhale. The inhale is about as long as the exhale and there should be no pause between them, so that the breathing proceeds in a natural, gentle cycle. The purpose of this pattern is to make the heartbeat harmonious, and the circulation of the blood and other bodily fluids more gentle. Psychologically, this form of breathing provides a feeling of harmony and love for all of creation. It also makes for greater sensitivity, sympathy and understanding toward others. (As mentioned above, this is the pattern which most resembles the predominant pattern in Rebirthing.)

Short Breaths

At the bodily level, the metabolism becomes faster and more irregular. Psychologically, it leads to quicker changes of thought and emotion, with a tendency to greater impatience and short temper. Spiritually, it leads to greater disharmony with the surrounding world, and to contradictory and subjective opinions.

4

Kundalini

There is, as yet, no scientific explanation for the reactions which occur during conscious breathing sessions, or for what controls the length of the energy cycle. The closest we can get is to compare Rebirthing phenomena with the reactions described in the various Eastern breathing exercises. So far, we have looked at some Chinese Chi Gong exercises. The other great area for comparison is yoga.

One major purpose of yoga exercises is to awaken the body's inner life energy – the kundalini. In order to expand consciousness and reach a higher state of mind, the body's own life energy has to be awakened and activated. According to Indian tradition, a person is not ready to experience altered states of consciousness before the kundalini is awake and allowed to flow freely in the body. The yoga trainee has to prepare the body and psyche to adjust properly to this expansion beyond the normal. The exercises of hatha yoga (physical yoga) and pranayama (breathing exercises) are especially designed for this purpose (see also pages 145–51).

The word kundalini comes from yoga, but there are similar concepts in most breathing techniques. The awakening of life-energy is an important factor in the various physical and psychological cleansing processes. When the body and mind have been cleared of blocks and 'impurities', the person will enter a new phase where body fluids flow so freely that more life-energy can be absorbed. This leads to an awakening of the body's kundalini, which in most adults is dormant. When the kundalini is released it produces an expansion of the mind, often resulting in the development of 'supernatural' abilities. This can include physical changes, for example less need for sleep and food, greater physical endurance and a capacity for self-healing.

Most descriptions of the awakening of kundalini are very similar, regardless of the cleansing method being used. The process can take anything from a couple of months to several years. One effect of the process is the experience of non-normal states of mind. These experiences go totally beyond everyday mental life, though they rarely result in a loss of contact with reality or disorientation severe enough to be called psychotic.

Accounts of the awakening of kundalini have many similarities with the reactions observed during Rebirthing sessions. Several scientific studies of the body's reactions to yoga exercises have been published. Here we will not, however, go into detail regarding the physical changes in the body. (Those interested should see, for example, James Funderburk, *Science Studies Yoga*, 1977.) We will concentrate here on descriptions of the various physical and psychological phenomena reported from the process of awakening kundalini in various yoga practices. Many of the symptoms and bodily reactions connected with the awakening of kundalini have been described by Sanella (1977). All of the following bodily sensations have also been observed in Rebirthing sessions, and may occur from the very first session. Experiences of expanded consciousness (e.g. visions, sounds, out-of-body) normally occur only after a person has completed at least ten sessions, and often at an even later stage. A precondition is that one should have cleared out a substantial part of biographical memory experiences. This normally involves having had at least one experience of birth memories. The examples listed below range from physical experiences to 'supernatural' phenomena, but they do not necessarily appear in this order.

Body Movements

The body often starts to move spontaneously. The movements vary greatly from person to person. They can be soft, curling, jerking, spastic or vibrating. The physiological explanation is that the breathing

43

exercise affects the cerebellum, the part of the brain that coordinates muscular movement.

Breathing

So-called spontaneous Rebirthing, with rapid shallow breathing, deep powerful breathing or spontaneous breathing patterns, occurs frequently. The practice of various breathing exercises may trigger a natural breathing cycle, which will normally be completed before returning to normal breathing. This spontaneous breathing reaction is originated in the hypothalamus, which monitors and controls the blood and its oxygen content. It does this by regulating the impulse to breathe.

Cramps

Various states of cramp occur often, affecting all parts of the body. They can last for a short period or persist over a longer time, affecting mobility. States of cramp are normally preceded by fear or hysterical states.

Body Sensations

The skin or the whole body is often felt to vibrate or itch. It is usually described as 'bubbles' in the body, or stitches and bubbling. Sometimes these experiences are perceived as sexual, similar to pre-orgasmic feelings. A physical explanation is that this is mainly caused by stimulation of the sensory cortex. This vibrational sensation often moves from the feet upwards (the way the kundalini is said to move through the body). The left big toe is often said to be the starting point. This toe has a direct link with the cerebral cortex. (The big toes play a special role in yoga exercises. Hindu mythology states that the holy river Ganges emerged out of the big toe of the Creator.)

Changes in Temperature

Body temperature can rapidly change from very hot to very cold. Sometimes, this is a purely subjective experience but there may also be objectively measurable changes in body temperature. A possible explanation is that when the kundalini force encounters a blockage in the body, friction is generated leading to localized temperature rise. This affects the hypothalamus which, in turn, will have effects on body temperature as a whole, causing rapid changes.

Experience of Pain

Sudden pain may be felt in the head, eyes, spine or other parts of the body without apparent reason. The pain usually remains for only short periods. A traditional explanation is that the kundalini force becomes intensively concentrated when passing through a 'blocked' part of the body. People who resist the process with a subconscious wish to retain control over the body are likely to experience these phenomena as painful.

Light and Sound Experiences

There are many descriptions of a wide range of light and sound experiences: colours flowing freely, illuminating or flowing from various parts of the body; voices, music, whistling or strong roaring or hissing. These phenomena may be caused by wave movements in the ventricles (cavities of the brain). This area influences the auditory cortex in the back lobe of the brain, which controls hearing and vision.

Emotional Experiences

Most emotional experiences are very intense, ranging from anxiety, fear, hate, depression and confusion to states of total bliss. The negative feelings are mostly experienced in the beginning of the session. They are later normally replaced by feelings of peace, harmony and love, at the end of a completely worked-through session. It is influence on the thalamus which probably causes these intense emotions. This area transports information to various centres in the cortex, in cooperation with the reticular and limbic systems. The latter has great impact on emotions and motivation.

Thought Experiences

People often report a change in the thought process itself. Thoughts pass through the mind faster or slower than usual and thought can even stop completely at times. Thoughts can also appear irrational, strange or unbalanced. These states can sometimes resemble mental illness, trance, impulsive actions or confusion.

Distancing

Another common experience is a feeling of separation from the actual event. 'What is happening has nothing to do with me.' This can also be described as being outside, observing the events, thoughts and feelings. This is known in yoga as 'witness consciousness'. In some cases, especially where there is an underlying imbalance in the person, this state may resemble schizophrenia. With the right type of guidance, it usually disappears rapidly and completely.

Out of Body Experiences

In this kind of experience one's own body appears distant. There is a feeling of being outside the body and the person can experience moving to various places while leaving the body behind. There is a sharp distinction between this type of experience and ordinary dreaming. The person can actually 'see' their own body from the outside, and be able to describe places without having physically been there. This distinguishes the phenomenon from dreaming or visualization.

Supernatural Experiences

In the latter stages of the kundalini process a capacity for 'supernatural' skills often appears. The most commonly occurring skills are clairvoyance, clairaudience and the ability to see the aura (the body's energy field) but other, even more remarkable skills may develop.

THE ORIGIN OF KUNDALINI

The concept of life energy being stored in the body is totally unknown to Western physiology. It is, however, one of the central ideas in the Eastern schools. They provide a thorough explanation both of its origin and its role in the body. In order to fully understand the importance of life-energy, it is essential to take a closer look at this explanation.

Kundalini, which is latent in the body, is said to be 'dormant' at the base of the spine. Kundalini energy is closely related to the reproductive instinct – the drive to express the immortality of a species. The symbol for kundalini is a snake curled three and a half times around a lingam (the holy phallus symbol representing the Indian supreme god, Shiva), inside a triangle facing downwards (the symbol for the female organ, called yoni, which represents the Indian goddess Shakti, meaning energy). In the Hindu tradition the god Shiva symbolizes the male cosmic principle and Shakti original nature and the feminine principle. Kundalini is the union between Shiva and Shakti which led to the origin of all species.

Kundalini is often described as something dangerous, great and powerful, which for the inexperienced can have negative consequences; something not totally within a person's own control. The fact that the body possesses such strong forces, about which we have little knowledge, is the starting point for Eastern cleansing processes. They treat such forces with respect, therefore the cleansing process is undertaken slowly and aims at a total preparation for each stage before it is entered into. Since we, in the Western world, generally lack this type of experience and are oriented towards quick results, we sometimes consider our time too precious to waste in patient preparations. This has led to frightful experiences for many people who have used drugs to reach altered states of consciousness. The process was too rapid, overwhelmed the body's natural defence mechanisms and flooded the system with negative kundalini energy, with horrible results.

The awakening of kundalini can also occur spontaneously without any apparent reason. Due to Western medicine's lack of experience and insight into these matters, experiences of this type can have devastating affects. They often lead to hospitalization and intensive drug treatment to curb the symptoms. No form of positive insight as to what has happened is provided (see also Part 4).

To describe kundalini in more detail one has to go back to the absolute beginning of the human being – the moment of conception. At the second division of cells after conception, four new cells are formed. Three of these grow rapidly into clusters of cells that form the base for the various parts of the body. One group forms the skin and nervous system, another forms the skeleton, muscles and blood circulation, and the third forms the food processing and respiratory organs. The fourth of the original cells grows much slower than the others and is therefore soon contained within the other three groups. It is this cluster which forms the genital organs.

The genital organs are, throughout the body's lifespan, in close contact with the pituitary gland. It is necessary to maintain a balance between these two poles in order for the body to function optimally. The genital organs have a special role in the body. They represent the drive within the species for immortality. Only cells from this part of the body can escape death by being brought out alive from the body and transferred over to a new living being at conception. This can occur in an endless chain.

Though kundalini is closely linked with sexuality and can be expressed through it, it is not identical with sexuality. It is rather the driving force behind sexuality. The power of kundalini is very active during a person's years of growth. It will gradually become dormant (curled up at the base of the spine). The average adult has to reawaken the kundalini force before it can be used actively in the body.

As soon as kundalini has been awakened, the dormant psychological energy stored in the lowest chakra (see pages 73-5) begins to move up towards the highest chakra at the top of the skull. The energy moves through the various chakras along the spine – the communication channels for all bodily sensations between the body and the head. From the head it continues down over the face, through the throat and ends in the abdomen. The kundalini in motion is better described as a concentration of energy that can be felt completely or partially by sensitive persons. This moving energy dissolves 'blocks of impurity or karma' in the body's fluid systems. This enables an increased amount of energy to flow through the body. As a result the cerebrospinal system (the brain and the spine) must radically expand. This gradual change in the system will also make it possible for consciousness to expand beyond its normal limits.

This expansion of the system will cause the central nervous system to rid itself of the blockages of unprocessed memories. When the awakened psychological energy encounters a blockage it spreads, penetrates and dissolves it. This can sometimes be a painful experience. When a blockage is dissolved the kundalini continues until it reaches the next one. Kundalini can also spread in various directions and work through blockages on several levels at the same time. Once the psychological energy has started to move upwards it can stop at a certain level but it will never return to its dormant position again.

5

An Interview With Leonard Orr, the Leading Exponent of the Rebirthing Movement

~~~

We shall conclude our overview of the power of breathing with some further explanations from the man who discovered this power through personal experience, and consequently developed the Rebirthing technique. The following is an extract from an interview with Leonard Orr conducted by the author in May 1989.

GUNNEL: Where did you get the original idea for Rebirthing? What was the beginning?

LEONARD: The ideas about Rebirthing came as a result of personal evolution. My first Rebirthing experience was actually in 1962. I was taking a bath and felt as if I couldn't get out. I did not have enough strength to get out of the bath. Of course I didn't understand what it was all about until years later. I had many 'bathtub experiences' like that between 1962 and 1968, but in 1968 I started having conscious birth memories when I was in my bathtub. And of course, in the years 1965 to 1967, I unravelled my 'death-urge'. ('Death-urge' is a special concept introduced by Leonard Orr. It is explained in full in Chapter 10.) This gave me a totally safe place in my mind and I felt safe in the physical universe. That safety enabled me to have more conscious memories of my birth.

The immortal energy has always been the basis of Rebirthing energy. It is no secret that rebirthers who have actually unravelled their death-urge and their birth-trauma (see page 103–7) produce very different benefits for their clients than rebirthers who are just breath-technicians. In a certain sense even expert breathing guides don't have the same depth to their intuition as rebirthers who have unravelled the birth-death cycle or at least a significant part of it. But it probably takes 50 to 100 years to really unravel your 'case' so that you are a pure expression of spirit.

The next development was a seminar I held in 1974 where I described my experiences of remembering my birth. The people there said they too wanted to have those kinds of experiences. So I suggested that they should get into their bathtubs and stay there until they felt they should get out. After that they should stay at least half an hour or an hour longer. There is an urgency barrier – a natural urgency barrier (see pages 141–3) – in the mind that keeps us from going too deep into ourselves. When people relax through that urgency-barrier they have fantastic realizations about themselves. These people from the seminar, had such powerful and dramatic experiences that they wanted me to be present with them when they were going through these experiences. That is where the idea of the rebirther came from. After watching a couple of people, I got the idea of using a snorkel and nose-clips in a big hot-tub, so that a couple of people could be in the water at the same time.

That is how Rebirthing really started. Guiding several hundred Rebirthing experiences, I noticed that people had a transformation of their breathing mechanism which I called 'the healing of the breath'. I wondered if it was possible to guide people into the breathing rhythm that I saw happen spontaneously during these experiences. I experimented and found that it was.

GUNNEL: What are the best conditions for a Rebirthing session? Do you need any special arrangements or can you do it anywhere and with anyone?

LEONARD: The best conditions are to have a private space and to be one on one. In some cases it is a good idea to have teams of three, consisting of the rebirther, an assistant and the rebirthee. It should be quiet so the rebirther can hear and guide the person's breathing rhythm for one to two hours, or however long it takes to have a completed energy cycle. Rebirthing is done in a reclining position so that the body is totally relaxed and the person can devote complete attention to the breathing rhythm. A session is a complete energy cycle. The time the session takes is determined by the energy itself. The person goes inside himself. Energy moves in the body as well as in the mind. There is a dissolving of negative energy concentrations, which has an emotional basis as well as a physiological basis.

The physical sensations that people experience can vary widely as well as the mental and spiritual experiences. In the beginning of the practice the energy cycles are more physical. But it is hard even to make that generalization because a person's internal experiences can be very different from the external appearance. But observing it objectively from the outside, there is more physiological action in the first five sessions or so, although internally it may be just the opposite. A person's physiological sensations might spark emotional fears and experiences inside, that preoccupy the person's rational mind so that they hardly even observe the physiological phenomena that they are going through.

I usually rebirth myself twice a day in water in my bathtub. It takes me half an hour to an hour or longer, twice a day to meditate and breathe. I experience that, by participating in the world, negative energy concentrates primarily in my solar plexus. I feel many layers of energy dissolving during these baths. It can be around my head, in my throat, in my ankles or other parts of my body, that I experience these negative energy concentrations. After meditating in the bath for half an hour or longer I just feel these letting go and my body relaxing. When I get out of the bath my body feels clear and clean. My energy body feels clean and balanced and gives me an experience of ecstasy and peace. Until I go to a shopping centre or somewhere and start to collect energy again. So if I can stay away from people, my energy body is clear all day except for a natural evolutionary cycle that takes place. Our energy changes throughout the day regardless of inputs. I bath twice a day to re-establish my balance.

The energy cycle is really the basis of Rebirthing. The first goal is to learn how to breathe energy as well as air. The second goal is to learn to breathe in water or to clean and balance the energy body on a daily basis with water and air. When people have learned that, they have a very powerful and practical healing tool that they can use to make their daily lives filled with ecstasy.

GUNNEL: Is it safe to do Rebirthing alone, or is it safe at all to do Rebirthing? Can it be dangerous?

LEONARD: Rebirthing as it relates to breathing is always safe. The breath is totally safe. The mind is not safe and the whole issue of safety brings up the idea of physical immortality (see pages 86–8). As long as a person believes that death, physical death, can happen to them without their control, that physical death is inevitable and beyond their control, they will never be safe no matter what they do. When you get rid of that idea and you feel safe in the universe as well as in your own mind and in the presence of God, there is nothing that is not safe. Everything is safe. So insecurity is created by the mind. When a person begins to understand their own mind, they don't have to worry about it any more. Rebirthing is only as safe as the person's mind. A person has to live in their body and mind whether they are breathing or not. If a person is unsafe they are unsafe whether they are doing Rebirthing or not.

GUNNEL: What is the most important part of the breathing in Rebirthing? The rhythm? The length of the breath or what?

LEONARD: The most important part is merging the inhale to the exhale. When you merge the inhale to the exhale you are experiencing the unity of being, on the physiological level. In a breath you are experiencing the merging of spirit and matter. I call it the biological experience of God.

GUNNEL: Is this something that you have developed yourself or is it based on old Eastern ideas?

LEONARD: No, I learned that, seeing people's breathing mechanism being transformed in early Rebirthing sessions. When I saw it I verbalized it as 'learning to breathe from the breath itself'. Learning to breathe from the breath itself is an internal realization for people at a certain point in the process. This experience was not induced in the beginning. It was a spontaneous experience. When I saw it happen, I asked myself if it was possible to induce that experience, by guiding a person's breathing rhythm into the rhythm I saw when it occurred spontaneously. I found that it was. But when I guided a person's breathing rhythm into that experience of learning from the breath itself, merging the inner breath with the outer breath, the person did not perceive what was happening. That is, they could not learn that breathing rhythm in two or three sessions. But a high percentage of people did learn that breathing rhythm. They learned the intuitive connection between the inner breath and the outer breath frequently in five to fifteen sessions. So there is a point at which a person notices that they are breathing energy as well as air. When that realization dawns upon the mind and soul of the individual, they have learned to breathe. That is what we mean when we call it conscious breathing. Conscious breathing is to consciously make that connection in the breathing rhythm. You merge the inhale with the exhale. That is the technique, but the power or the spirit of the technique is the intuitive knowledge that you are breathing energy as well as air. Intuitive awareness of energy as well as air.

GUNNEL: In pranayama they emphasize the pause between inhale and exhale. In Rebirthing it is the opposite?

LEONARD: The connected breathing is the natural form of breathing the spirit into the body. Newborn babies breathe that way. People breathe that way in the middle of deep sleep. That is not to say that there isn't some value in doing some different kinds of exercises. I particularly believe in alternated nasal breathing. That is inhaling through one nostril and exhaling through the other in an alternated way. That particular exercise cleanses the passages from the nostrils into the nervous system. When those passages are cleaned, energy is integrated in the body in a way that heals and maintains all the organs.

GUNNEL: How do you guide people through a session? Is it just the intuitive experience or is it both that and the actual technique?

LEONARD: People are so constructed that if you only use the technique of merging the inhale with the exhale, the experience will take place in most people spontaneously. The skill of a good rebirther is determined by their intuition. To be able to see, to hear and to feel the energy merging with the air. Training people in intuition is not possible. In that sense Rebirthing is not a technique. It is an inspiration beyond technique. People can ultimately only learn intuition through inner realization. You can provide an environment for people to learn intuition, but there is no way to train people in intuition. You can only provide an environment in which a person can develop their intuition. It is possible to observe when a person does develop that intuitive skill but there is no way you can force it.

GUNNEL: What is the difference between cold water, hot water and dry sessions, if any?

LEONARD: Big difference. Warm water stimulates womb memories and deep psycho-analytical and psycho-physiological experiences. It induces a state of very deep relaxation. Our whole physical body was formed in the medium of warm water in the womb. So our basic emotional structure is formed in the medium of hot water. Birth is the first experience of cold. Cold water Rebirthing has a tendency to dissolve our temperature trauma and other unpleasant experiences of coming out of the warm womb into the cold world. Cold water Rebirthing has a way of Rolfing the energy body. (Rolfing is a kind of deep tissue massage developed by Ida Rolf and used to evoke emotions through physical contact.) Rolfing is a way of stimulating and realizing pain that is stored in the psycho-physiological organism. The deepest levels of pain in the human organism can be stimulated and realized through cold water Rebirthing. The basic technique of cold water Rebirthing is to go in, one inch at a time, into the water and to integrate the sensations before going in the next inch. It could take half an hour to one hour to get into the water. The water can be any temperature as long as it is water and not ice so that you can get into it. But the air temperature should not be below freezing, otherwise you could freeze to death. The more comfortable the air temperature the better. I prefer to do it in the middle of the day, when there is a lot of sun and a blue sky. Bright sunlight enables you to integrate pain and discomfort and stimulates the release more rapidly. But I have done cold water Rebirthing in rain storms when people were using umbrellas.

GUNNEL: Why is Rebirthing so effective? How does it affect the body?

LEONARD: The ultimate meaning of that question is why do human beings breathe. Human beings breathe to inhale oxygen physiologically and to release waste material. In fact, breathing is the biggest excretory system of the body. Sweating is the next most significant and urination and defecation come last, way down the list in relation to releasing the waste of the body. When you are doing the connected breathing rhythm you are producing energy flows in the body, that nourish and clean it more effectively, on an optimal level.

Part 2

THE PHYSIOLOGY OF BREATHING

6

A Physiological Explanation of Breathing

When breath control is perfected,
the body becomes light,
countenance becomes cheerful,
eyes become bright,
digestive power increases,
and it brings internal purification and joy.

Grahayamalatantra, chapter 13

Breathing can involve much more than simply providing oxygen for the body. Despite the obvious fact that breathing is the essential life-giving mechanism for the body, little interest in the West has been shown in studying and fully comprehending its potential. Most adults do not utilize the total capacity of their lungs. Yet virtually no concern has been expressed as to why this should be so, what effect it has on the body, or how this can be corrected. The main interest shown so far in this area has been concerned with how to improve the physical ability of the body in relation to sports performance. A great deal still needs to be done to establish the importance of increased breathing for physical and psychological diseases.

The purpose of breathing, according to Western physiology, is to take oxygen into the body and convey waste products out of it. It is seen as a purely physiological function. In Eastern physiology, however, a secondary, inner system is identified, which provides the body's supply of life-energy (Sanskrit *prana*, Chinese *chi*, Japanese *ki*, Tibetan *thig-le* or *rlung*). Life-energy is a concept that has not been recognized in the West – at least not until relatively recently. Eastern schools, however, distinguish an 'inner breathing' – one so deep and total that it opens up the entire body permitting an inflow of life-energy to permeate every cell. It may be this aspect of breathing which actually holds the key to our well-being.

To get a clear picture of all the aspects of breathing, it will be helpful to have an understanding of the basic physiological functions involved in the respiratory process.

Oxygen is the single most important substance for the body. It is essential to every cell in the body to produce energy necessary to sustain life. We bring oxygen into the body when we inhale and give off the body's by-products when we exhale. This is done through the breathing apparatus of the body which consists of:

The upper respiratory tract with
- nose
- mouth
- pharynx
- larynx
- trachea

The lungs and diaphragm with
- bronchi
- bronchioles
- alveoli
- capillaries

When we breathe, we inhale air through the nose, which is the natural pathway by which air enters the body. The nose is divided into two narrow cavities by a partition, the septum, made of bone and cartilage. The outer end of the cavities, the nostrils, are lined with fine hairs that filter out dust and bacteria from the air. The septum is covered by a mucous membrane which moistens and warms up the air. If too many particles accumulate on the membrane a sneezing spasm will be triggered. The two cavities, the nasal fossae, are very narrow, less than 6mm wide. The cavity at the back of the nose is divided into long thin sections by three ridges of bone. The passage is lined with mucous membrane with a rich blood supply. Here the inhaled air is moistened and warmed up. This membrane secretes 0.5l of mucus per day. The sinuses or cavities in the front of the skull are connected with the nose. They form a triangle behind the eyebrows and the cheeks on each side of the nose.

After being inhaled through the nostrils, the air passes through the pharynx, the cavity at the back of the mouth that links the nose with the mouth, and then down to the larynx and trachea. In the pharynx area the co-ordination of the swallowing and breathing is achieved by the pharyngeal plexus. This activity is controlled from the lower brain stem. The main role of the larynx, as regards breathing, is to assist the vocal cords in using breath to produce sounds. The upper part of the trachea is at the front of the throat. The trachea is about 10cm long and 2.5cm wide. From the trachea the air continues down into the thoracic cavity in the neck, where the left and right bronchi pass it on to the respective sides of the lungs. The trachea and bronchi are held open, like hollow tubes, by cartilaginous rings in their walls. The mucous membrane in the entry to the lungs moistens the trachea and bronchi. It is covered with hair-like cilia, which function as traps for particles of dirt in the incoming air. The cilia move in an upward direction that sweeps the particles back up into the mouth. If too many particles accumulate, they trigger a coughing spasm.

The bronchi divide down into smaller and smaller branches, secondary and tertiary bronchi, leading to even smaller tubes, called bronchioles. These, in turn, lead to clusters of air-filled sacs, called alveoli. There are around 750 million of these air sacs. The pulmonary arteries form a second system of tubes, as they enter the lungs alongside the bronchi. The smaller tubes all contain blood vessels as they run alongside the bronchioles. At the alveoli they form capillaries. This is where the gas exchange with the blood actually occurs. The capillaries are so narrow that the blood cells pass through them in single file. This enables the blood cells to be exposed to oxygen all over their surfaces. Oxygen is taken up by the haemoglobin in the blood. At the same time, the red blood cells discharge carbon dioxide back into the alveoli, for further transportation out of the body through exhalation. From the alveoli the blood, now enriched with oxygen, flows to the left chamber of the heart, which pumps it to all the parts of the body. The oxygen in combination with elements of the food we eat (now in liquid form) is transported out to the cells. At each cell these nutrients are exchanged for waste products in the cell, in the form of carbon dioxide. This is then carried back to the lungs by the blood in a never-ending circle. The oxygenized blood from the heart vitalizes, nourishes and strengthens the body. On the way out from the heart the blood is bright red and vital, filled with life-giving qualities. On its way back it is like a sewage ditch filled with the waste products of the body.

The two lungs form a movable, elastic organ that takes up most of the thorax. Each lung can move freely in any direction except at the root, which mainly consists of the tubes and arteries that connect it to the windpipe and heart. Between the lungs there is a space containing:

the nerves of the breast cavity
blood and lymphatic vessels
windpipe, food pipe and heart

The average lungs of an adult person weigh from one kilo to one and a half kilo. The different sides of the lungs vary slightly in size, the right one being the larger, as the heart takes up some of the space in the left side of the thorax. Each lung is divided into lobes. The right lung is divided into three lobes, the left into two. The lungs are spongy and porous with a very elastic tissue which, if flattened out, would cover around one hundred square metres. They are covered by a double layer of smooth membrane, like a strong bag. This is connected to the lungs at one side, and to the inside of the chest cavity at the other. Between the membranes a fluid is excreted which makes it possible for the surfaces to glide against each other without friction. This fluid also holds the lungs open by surface tension. (Like a drop of water can hold two sheets of glass together, so that they can only be separated by a sideways, sliding movement.) If the lungs were removed from the chest they would collapse like deflated balloons. The lungs are pulled out when the chest is expanded. When we exhale, the rib muscles relax gradually. Otherwise the lungs would spring back immediately, provided that they are not kept empty on purpose. If air gets in between the lung and the wall, the surface tension breaks, and the lungs collapse.

The breathing mechanism is initiated and co-ordinated by the respiratory centre in the medulla oblongata, or hindbrain. It is normally an automatic function that operates on information from nerve feedbacks in the lungs and muscles and from the oxygen-carbon dioxide balance in the blood. The signals are initiated according to the level of carbon dioxide in the blood, rather than the amount of oxygen present. But it can also be triggered by emotions and controlled by the will. One group of nerve cells in this centre initiates inhalation and another exhalation. Inhalation is an active process, based on an impulse from the vagus nerves, exhalation is the reverse, a relaxation of the muscles involved, caused by inhibition of the impulse. Air is brought into the lungs in two ways, which are mainly complementary. One is via the piston-like up-down movement of the diaphragm, the big cupola-formed muscle that stretches over the ribcage and separates the chest cavity from the abdomen. The movement of the diaphragm is almost as automatic as the movement of the heart muscle, except that the diaphragm can also be affected by the will. When the muscle expands the volume of the lungs is increased, which causes air to rush into the vacuum created. When the muscle relaxes, the lung volume decreases and the air is forced out. The alternative method of bringing air into the lungs is by contraction of the intercostal muscles that surround the chest. This contraction makes the chest expand, producing the same effect as the movement of the diaphragm muscle.

'Ordinary', or non-aroused breathing, involves around 12 breaths per minute. During heavy physical exercises the rate can increase to up to 80 breaths per minute. Average conscious breathing in a Rebirthing session is around twenty to thirty breaths per minute, although the volume of the inhaled air may be up to ten times more than in ordinary breathing. Oxygen makes up about a fifth of the air we breathe. During 24 hours we breathe approximately 8000 litres of air and 17.5 litres of blood pass through the lung capillaries. Some of the body's cells are able to function for a while without oxygen. The brain, however, cannot be without oxygen at all.

The cells use a combination of oxygen and sugar as 'fuel' to produce energy. This is the reason why the waste products consist of carbon dioxide and water. Breathing is one of the most important ways for the body to eliminate waste products. Only 3 per cent of the body's total waste products are eliminated through the faeces, 7 per cent though the urine and 20 per cent through the skin. The remaining 70 per cent of the body's waste products are eliminated through exhalation. If a human being does not breathe enough fresh air, the blood cannot be completely cleaned. This means that waste products, which should have been eliminated during oxygenation, are being brought back into the body. Instead of enriching and rebuilding the body, the blood is conveying toxins around the system. This can be compared to being poisoned by polluted air.

HYPERVENTILATION

Breathing closely reflects our psychic condition. The commonest reaction to powerful emotional experiences is to restrict breathing. The body's defence systems are oriented towards the shutting out of all physically and psychologically painful experiences. The body does this to avoid overloading its various systems. Restriction of breathing is one of the main mechanisms for achieving this defensive reaction. Breathing becomes shorter and shallower until it stops almost completely. In situations where extremely powerful and threatening physical or emotional experiences are encountered this 'shutting out' mechanism may be overwhelmed. In such cases a person may spontaneously begin to hyperventilate. This is an intensified breathing rhythm which, at times, appears strikingly similar to Rebirthing, but with the important difference that it is accompanied by anxiety rather than relaxation.

At every breath the diaphragm muscle is active during inhalation. On exhalation the air is pushed out by relaxation of the diaphragm muscle, which returns to a resting position. If exhalation is forced, by actively pushing the diaphragm muscle, hyperventilation can result.

During forced exhalation more carbon dioxide than normal is exhaled. This means that the level of carbon dioxide in the blood goes below a certain threshold value, which has the effect of suspending automatic regulation of breathing by the brain. This occurs in the brain centre which controls the inhalation signals to the respiratory muscles. When the stimulation from this centre stops, the body spontaneously stops breathing, which in turn leads to a general alerting of the body's defence mechanisms and a state of panic is experienced. The panic often causes people to seek medical attention. The treatment is, however, extremely simple. The patient is told to breathe into some kind of container (the hands, a paper bag, etc). Doing this causes the exhaled air, with its high content of carbon dioxide, to be inhaled again. The level of carbon dioxide is soon restored, which will restart the signals from the brain's breathing centre.

Rebirthing is often confused with hyperventilation. There is a precise distinction between the correct breathing pattern in a Rebirthing session and hyperventilation. There are, however, often situations during a Rebirthing session which may cause the person to fall into a hyperventilation pattern. This is certainly not intended and a good therapist will know how to prevent this. Breathing during Rebirthing should really be called 'super-breathing' – an optimal method of breathing. It will not cause hyperventilation, regardless of the speed and intensity of the breathing, as long as the relaxed exhale is maintained. The body may experience intense physical sensations, vibrations, or tinglings during Rebirthing; this, however, is generally perceived as positive and pleasant.

A doctor in a hospital casualty department, who is also a trained Rebirthing therapist, has successfully guided hyperventilating patients into Rebirthing sessions, as an alternative to conventional treatment, for this condition. He has guided the patient's breathing into a relaxed and connected pattern, until the patient has come through the acute attack of anxiety that caused the hyperventilation. In all cases the patients have left hospital, calm and balanced, without having to take any tranquillizing medicine.

ALKALOSIS

If a forced exhale is maintained for long enough, the acid-base level of the blood is adjusted to the lowered level of carbon dioxide and a state called alkalosis occurs. This is characterized by cramps and muscular spasms and can lead to intense pain in the tensed muscles and joints.

In Rebirthing alkalosis can sometimes occur, especially during the first sessions when one is still not fully familiar with the process. The body's natural defence mechanism will try, unconsciously, to restrict the breathing and to emphasize the exhalation. As soon as the breathing returns to a relaxed pattern the cramps will dissolve, often leading to powerful vibrations and tickling sensations throughout the body. If the cramps are not dissolved immediately, they will disappear at the end of the energy cycle when the breathing spontaneously returns to its normal pattern.

Cramp occurs most frequently in the hands, around the mouth or over the entire face. One explanation for this may be that these areas are closely linked with our self-perception and how we relate to others. Both the hands and the mouth are important for our communication with others. The hands are a mode of expression for our creativity and can be used to express a vast range of feelings and thoughts. The mouth is the outer part of our speech apparatus – our most important mode of communication. What the mind represses (because it is perceived as threatening) cannot be talked about – it would first have to be brought into consciousness. Loss of control in these areas is perceived as extremely threatening by the body's defence system and it will react powerfully to prevent this.

THE BRAIN

The brain cannot go without oxygen for more than a very short time before being irreversibly damaged. The brain needs a constant wash through with oxygen-rich blood to maintain its normal functions. To 'oxygen-flood' the brain through increased breathing, as in a conscious breathing session, has been shown to have a very positive effect on the brain. This can be established through the many subjective reports of, for instance, 'increased creativity' and 'clearer thoughts' which have been gathered over the years. But, so far, no systematic research has been done on the specific effects of conscious breathing on the brain. Certain deductions can, however, be made from existing brain research, which does include work on the effects of breathing in general. First, though, it's necessary to consider the structure of the brain.

The human brain consists of billions of nerve cells, called neurones, joined together by a supporting network of so-called glia cells. Each nerve cell has many dendrites which receive and pass on information. A single cell can have connections with more than 10,000 other cells. The total number of connections in the brain is, therefore, virtually incalculable. Many of the neurones have long fibrous connections with distant parts of the body. Information is transmitted up to the brain from the body's different receivers in the form of chemically-coded impulses. This information is received, decoded and analyzed by the brain's dense network of neurones.

The intricate web of nerves that constitutes the human nervous system weighs only three and a half pounds yet is probably the most complex system known in the universe. And, by the awe and wonderment it produces, it is for some the most beautiful.

Russell, Explaining the Brain, 1975

Conventional wisdom has long asserted that brain cells cannot be renewed. Even if this were true, the brain has such vast numbers of neurones that even after 80 years, a normal individual would have lost only about 1% of his/her brain cells. Moreover, recent research evidence has contradicted the conventional view: brain cells have just the same capacity to continually renew themselves as the other cells of the body. In addition to this, the number of connections between brain cells steadily increases over an individual's lifespan. The consequence of both these processes is that, in reality, human mental capacities steadily increase with time.

The brain is structured in two halves. According to current theory, the right side of the brain is non-verbal and intuitive. It thinks in patterns and images and requires totalities for comprehension. It does not understand chains of deductive reasoning, statistics, letters or words, and lacks a conception of time. The right side of the brain is the seat of wisdom, in its traditional sense. It is often referred to as the mystical side of the brain. It seems to have some sort of inexplicable rapport with the cosmos as a whole.

The left side of the brain is responsible for the rest of humankind's mental activity; that is to say, rational thought, deductive logic, calculation, etc. All information here is reduced to its component parts before being processed. Both sides of the brain register their respective images of experience and store their own memories.

In an ideally healthy person the two sides of the brain are fully integrated: there is free access for their different and complementary types of information to be exchanged. In a neurotic person, on the other hand, there are blocks between these two spheres: emotional and rational experience cannot be meaningfully linked together. The neurotic reacts emotionally in certain situations without understanding why.

Until recently the intuitive right side of the brain was not valued as highly as the rational left side. This is a consequence of the traditional, Western ideal of life, and its excessive stress on the mental characteristics of the left side of the brain. But during the last decade or so, this cultural bias has begun to crumble under the impact of research into the mechanisms of thinking and creativity. The right side is now credited as the originator of new, creative ideas – including many in science and mathematics. A new, intellectual respect for its cosmic wisdom has appeared.

The brain's structure can also be divided according to the evolutionary stages represented in its present form. A few distinct structures can be identified according to this criterion:

The spinal cord is the oldest part of the brain. The first growth of the brain occurs in the foetus at approximately 8 weeks of age and this accelerates to a spurt of maximum growth just before birth.

Consequently, the brain is most impressionable and receptive to outer impressions at this period in its development.

The brain stem which is the top part of the spinal cord contains the reticular formation, which is a concentration of nerves controlling wakefulness and monitoring information from the various senses.

The cerebellum is also connected with the brain stem and is the part of the brain that coordinates information from the senses with muscular activity in order to make movement as smooth and precise as possible.

The midbrain on top of the brain stem, which includes the thalamus and the limbic system (the seat of the emotions), functions as the gate to consciousness. Here, different impulses from the other parts of the brain are integrated with each other. Physical and psychological experiences which are so painful that they cannot be integrated by the brain's cortex are here directed along other pathways in the brain. This type of redirection can result in projections and false associations, for example the paranoid hallucination that strangers in the street are whispering about us. It can also lead to compulsions, such as being a 'workaholic', or the obsessive pursuit of hobbies in order to escape from reality.

The cortex covers the midbrain. Seventy-five per cent of all the body's neurones are concentrated in the cortex. It has a high density of blood vessels, which gives it a greyer colour than the rest of the brain. In the cortex there are various areas that control various functions, for example, the motor cortex for movements, and the sensory cortex for body sensations, areas for language, smell and taste. The frontal part, or the frontal lobes, are the seats of consciousness. It is here that impulses from smell, feeling and movements are integrated with impressions from our inner world. It is here that unconscious material is transformed into conscious thought or our conceptions and impressions of the inner and outer world are constructed.

BRAIN HORMONES

Up until around 1975 there was a general consensus among researchers that the brain was a 'dry computer', operating with electricity as its driving force. Now, however, many are convinced that the brain is, in reality, a giant gland which dispenses hormones and has receptors for hormones (Bergland, 1985). It is bathed in hormones and a constant stream of hormones flows up and down its nerve fibres. Every event in the brain is intimately connected with hormone activity. It has been established that these 'brain hormones' are exactly the same as those produced in the other, better-known glands of the body. This implies that the mechanisms which underlie thought operate in the same way throughout the body and are not confined to the brain. In other words, our memories are not just stored in the brain but throughout the body. This, it can be assumed, is the reason why a sudden release of stored memories can be triggered by a conscious breathing pattern. As mentioned before, the 'flushing' of the body's circulatory systems during Rebirthing obviously brings a lot of hormones or chemical particles from all parts of the body into circulation through the body and brain.

Hormone release is associated with marked changes in bodily state – for example, when we laugh, cry, or take exercise. Many researchers today are convinced that hormones are the key to all of the brain's activities: it is they which mediate our experiences of satisfaction, love, appetite, joy, sleep, pain, sex, grief, anxiety and many, many other psychological states. An 'abnormal mix' of hormones can give rise to pathological conditions, such as senility or depression. It is now known, for example, that depression is associated with enormous changes in the endocrine system.

On the other hand, hormones also have a vital role in the body's healing processes. Pain releases a complex endocrinal condition. There are hormones stored in the brain which are far more effective in the treatment of pain than anything currently available to medical science. Norman Cousins (1978) refers to 'happiness hormones', which have curative properties. It is unknown exactly how or where in the body these hormones are produced or how they are activated, but it now seems clear that they play a significant part in the body's 'miraculous' ability to heal itself, as recorded in religious 'myths' and anecdotal evidence.

Knowledge about how hormones control different types of

behaviour is the key to the more effective use of the brain and to knowing how to turn on the body's healing systems. During meditation, it has been possible to detect the release of 'harmony giving' hormones, although little is known about their composition and mode of operation. The brain has the largest turnover of chemical substances of all the body's organs. It is constantly producing proteins in order to sustain its mental activities: the more mentally active a person is, the more rapid his or her protein synthesis is.

THE BREATHING BRAIN

Of all the body's organs the brain requires the largest blood supply. The brain contains millions of tiny blood vessels which supply every cell with oxygen and nutrition. The brain consumes 25 per cent of the body's oxygen supply, despite the fact that it constitutes only 3 per cent of the body's total weight. If the blood supply is reduced, brain functions will suffer. For example, elderly people can suffer a 50 per cent blockage in the arteries supplying the brain because of calcification. It has proved possible to raise their IQ significantly by cleaning out the arteries, thereby increasing the oxygen supply to their brains. Significant intellectual vitalization of older people can also be brought about very rapidly, by supplying the brain with an increased concentration of oxygen in special oxygen tents.

During brain surgery, it has been observed that brain volume is altered by breathing. The volume is reduced during inhalation and increased during exhalation. During normal breathing the brain moves approximately 18 times per minute. A radically increased frequency of breathing can therefore be compared with a massage of the brain. Increased breathing frequency also gives an increased flow of oxygen-enriched blood to the brain and produces a complete flushing out of its accumulated waste products. The capillaries expand and, most significantly, the pineal gland and the pituitary gland are influenced.

The blood–brain barrier functions like a sluice gate in the brain. It is a sophisticated mechanism for pumping in certain things and pumping others out. It is not yet fully understood how the blood–brain barrier functions, but it is known that it enables the brain to pick and choose amongst the enormous number of hormones which are continually flowing through it. If it proves to be the case that the blood-brain barrier opens and shuts itself selectively, it could lead to a totally new understanding of many aspects of normal behaviour. The sexual orgasm, for example, could be the result of a temporary opening of the brain's capillaries which allow blood-borne 'happiness hormones' to come into the brain. The flushing out which occurs through a raised breathing frequency (as in a Rebirthing session) can lead to a similar effect. Depression could be brought about by a malfunction of the mechanism, which prevents happiness hormones getting through to the brain.

AN EASTERN EXPLANATION OF THE BODY'S FUNCTIONS

Western medicine's description of the human body and its physiology was originally derived from observations made during the dissection of dead bodies. It is based on the idea of a separation between the body and soul, which leads to the conclusion that the body can only be studied externally. The body's physiology is limited to observable phenomena. The Eastern description is based on both objective studies and subjective experiences of the body's functions, encountered during altered states of consciousness. Given this perspective, Eastern physiology includes a subjective dimension of the body that cannot be obtained by merely studying the inner organs.

The Eastern schools differ only slightly in their descriptions of the body's functions. The following is based on the Indian yoga school.

Whereas Western schools divide physiology into a mental and physical function, Indian yoga theory distinguishes between five different bodies or functions:

A physical body
An energy or prana body

A mental body
An intuitive mental body
A bliss body

This structure is designed to illustrate the body's ability to absorb prana (life-giving energy). In the air, the foods and the liquids that the body needs, there is a life-giving essence which is essential for the body's survival, and which the body is able to extract. To be able to receive fully the life-giving substance in the air, a person has to breathe fully, in a manner relaxed enough to maintain an openness and receptivity in all five bodies. This is known as 'inner breathing'. It is this optimal breath that revitalizes and restores the body and psyche. By refinement of the body's functions, through specially designed cleansing exercises, the capacity to obtain inner breathing can be increased. This has a rejuvenating effect and facilitates the awakening of the kundalini forces.

The body is surrounded by a magnetic energy-field, the aura, which is affected by the physical and mental state of the body. It can be compared with a person's character or personality. One of the functions of the aura is to transfer to the body the supply of energy present in the rays of the sun from electromagnetic radiation in the air.

The human body has, apart from the circulatory systems known to Western science, a network of around 72,000 energy channels (Sanskrit *nadis*, Chinese *ching luo* or meridians). Their purpose is to transport life energy (prana) to all parts of the body. These channels have seven major junctions (chakras) located along the spine, from its base to the crown of the head. The chakras' locations correspond to the main inner organs and the various nerve centres. The different schools identify different numbers of chakras. The yoga school identifies seven chakras. The Tibetan school combines the crown chakras, thus counting only five chakras in the whole body. A chakra can be described as a whirlpool of energy. The flow of energy in the various chakras causes a counterflow, the aura. Every chakra vibrates at a certain frequency which is reflected in the human psyche and experienced as levels of consciousness. When the energy in the chakras is balanced, it is reflected in a balanced psyche.

The lowest chakra, at the base of the spine, is known as the first chakra. It is concerned in its mental aspect with physical safety. The seventh, or the highest chakra, reflects a sense of enlightenment and cosmic union. It is possible to be unbalanced in a certain chakra, and this will be expressed in behaviour. An imbalance in the first chakra, for example, will make a person largely concerned with personal safety. People may have reached different levels of balance for various areas in life, especially those who have developed specific talents.

According to many yoga masters, most people today are unbalanced in their lower chakras. This can be seen in selfish endeavours to satisfy physical needs, and in their lack of spiritual insight or sense of oneness with the universe. This, in turn, may lead to destructive behaviour expressed in conflicts and war.

The chakras have been named according to their special qualities and their various effects on the human psyche. They are described here from the lowest, first chakra upwards.

1. *Muladhara* (root support) Imbalance results in a desire for personal safety as the highest goal. It is located at the base of the spine and corresponds to the pelvic plexus, testes and ovaries.

2. *Swadhisthana* (one's own place) Imbalance produces an exaggerated desire for personal and sensual pleasure. It is located just below the navel and corresponds to the hypogastric plexus, adrenal glands and kidneys.

3. *Manipura* (gem city) This is linked with drives for power. It is located just above the navel and corresponds to the solar plexus, liver and pancreas.

4. *Anahata* (unstruck sound) Balance here develops creativity and unconditional love. It is located in the heart region and corresponds to the cardiac plexus and thymus gland.

5. *Vishuddha* (purity centre) Balance in this chakra facilitates the integration of events and the development of inner harmony. It is located in the throat area and corresponds to the pharyngeal plexus and thyroid gland.

6 *Ajna* (non-knowledge) Balance in the Ajna can enable Siddhi-abilities (ESP). It is located between the eyes ('the third eye') and corresponds to the naso-ciliary plexus and pituitary gland.

7 *Sahasrara* (the thousand-petalled centre) Balance here can bring about a union of all the levels of consciousness with the highest, known as enlightenment. It is located at the top of the head and corresponds to the cerebrum and the pineal gland.

7

Breathing as a Therapy for Organic Disease

INTRODUCTION

Rebirthing is claimed by many to be a very effective way to cure physical illness. This statement does, however, need clarification, so as not to give a misleading picture of the very essence of Rebirthing's philosophy. It is important to point out here that Rebirthing is *a very efficient tool to awaken and reinforce the healing power within a person*. In other words it is not the *technique* but rather *the person breathing* who is responsible for the healing process. The whole idea behind Rebirthing is to make the rebirthee aware of his personal responsibility in the healing process. It is therefore essential to provide some form of insight into the mechanisms that cause illness and why illness occurs. Unless a person understands the concept of underlying psychological factors driving disease, the curing of one illness may well lead only to the onset of another. This understanding can be divided into a physical and a psychological approach. We will firstly deal with the physical side by looking briefly at Western medicine's present position and attitude to the curing of organic disease, and compare it with the holistic approach of the various Eastern medical traditions.

Western medicine has developed within the mechanical world view put forward by Newton, Darwin and Descartes. Human beings are seen, more or less, as machines, with interchangeable parts. As the focus is on how to cure illness, rather than why it occurs, illness tends to be isolated from the rest of a person's inner and outer life. This approach brings with it a craving to invent new and more sophisticated technology to maintain an optimal performance for the body. Transplants and donation of organs are seen as ultimate medical achievements. Drugs are produced for almost every purpose in life. Behind this leading edge of medical technology lies a whole spectrum of disharmonious living. Modern life seems to gather us up into a frenzied world of stressful living, in which the very basis of our life on this planet, our natural environment, becomes undermined. The pollution and destruction of the environment is accompanied by the disharmonious lifestyle of the individual: inertia, poor diet and a life-threatening build up of toxins in the body from highly-processed food. The body's immune system loses its power of discrimination and the individual's natural ability for self-healing and recovery comes under threat.

THE HOLISTIC APPROACH

During the last decades this absurdity has become obvious to many in the medical profession, who are now searching for alternatives that will develop human potential in harmony with nature. Such healing methods are based on a holistic approach, where the whole of the patient's life situation is reviewed before a diagnosis is made.

Although new to the Western world, the holistic approach in medicine has been applied for at least three thousand years in the Indian ayurvedic medicine (Sanskrit: *ayur* meaning health; *veda* meaning knowledge). The basic principle of ayurvedic medicine is the equal stress it places on the physical, psychological and spiritual points of view. To this is added the theory of tridosha (the three elements) that link human beings with cosmic forces. The elements or humours are wind, bile and phlegm. Of the three, wind (prana) has the dominant position. Prana influences all bodily functions. Prana is subdivided into various functions: 'apana' influences the region of the anus, acting downwards, controlling urine and faeces, the sexual organs, etc; 'samana' in the region of the navel, controls digestion, etc; 'udana' in the throat, controls speech, etc, and 'vyana' pervades all parts of the body. Illness occurs when any of the humours is agitated in relation to the others, thereby causing imbalance. Ayurvedic cures often include advice about diet and living conditions in addition to various cleansing exercises, such as yoga and breathing exercises.

In Chinese traditional medicine, the doctor's role is to keep the patient well and not just cure him when illness has already occurred. In early times the doctor was paid as long as the 'patient' remained well; the doctor was seen as failing in his work if the patient got ill. If this idea was applied to Western medicine, it could have a substantial effect on the progress of health care. As the situation is today, physicians would be out of work if everyone was healthy. In this sense, there is an incentive for physicians to surround themselves with sick people. (The importance of attitudes is discussed further in the Part 3.)

In ancient Chinese theory, illness is ascribed to an imbalance in the body and psyche. The yin and yang forces in the body are not balanced (see Part 4). Diagnoses are made through a highly developed system of interpreting the pulse and urine samples. Treatment consists, as in ayurvedic medicine, of breathing exercises, acupuncture, diet and general advice, all aimed at restoring the body's balance.

Traditional Tibetan medicine makes no real distinction between religion and medicine. Instead it identifies three different aspects of human existence on earth: Dharma, representing the religious aspect of human life; Tantra, standing for the various body and mind cleansing processes, and the Somatic aspect or body aspect where medicine belongs.

These traditional medicines have all now been restored in their respective countries. They were put aside because of their short-comings in providing instant cures for certain types of disease, a capacity of which Western medicine is most proud. In recent years traditional medicine has also come to serve as a model for the holistic approach in the West.

Many Western physicians have begun to study these ancient schools of medicine and have tried to apply them to Western medicine. One result is that acupuncture has become recognized as a valid form of treatment. Yoga and meditation have been prescribed as therapy for patients suffering from stress. Colours have been chosen for their healing qualities in the colour schemes for the decoration of hospitals. Music, autosuggestion, relaxation, meditation and various forms of visualization have been used to facilitate the healing process for various diseases. Terminal cancer patients are one group that has particularly benefited from this type of treatment.

In some cases, the psychological healing process has been initiated, while the patient is still under the influence of anesthetics. The doctor, while performing the operation, tells the patient about the body's natural ability for self-healing. It has been established that the patient can register, on an unconscious level, what happens during the operation and can later give an account of this during hypnosis. The impressions have been registered in the brain without first being processed in consciousness. The effect on the body can, in this situation, be greater than that achieved by talking to a conscious person. Patients receiving positive feedback while under anesthetic have been shown to experience a quick and uncomplicated healing process.

A Personal Experience

I have only had a general anesthetic once in my life. After the operation, which in itself was totally uncomplicated, I had an unpleasant feeling of having lost my memory. There seemed to be a gap in my life which felt unsettling in a vague way. It was an irritating feeling which I could not get rid of. A couple of months later I experienced, during a breathing session, a dream-like sequence, where I was back on the operation table. In a detached way I saw and heard what was happening around me. There was nothing particularly dramatic, but afterwards, the feeling of a time-gap in my mind had gone completely.

MATERNITY HOSPITALS

Another area where medical attitudes have undergone a major change in recent years is birth. This is closely linked with a growing understanding of the importance of imprints from the earliest phase of life. This attitude first emerged with Otto Rank (1929) but has had its greatest influence from recently-developed therapies which enable regression to the time of birth or earlier (Rebirthing being one of them). These give the adult person a chance to re-experience their birth trauma (see Part 3).

One tendency in the changing attitude to birth is a move away from the 'sick patient in hospital' model to one of supporting the mother and restoring the natural process. Many maternity hospitals now teach special breathing techniques as an alternative to drugs. A beneficial result of this has been to break the vicious circle of fear–pain complication. Mothers are also encouraged to try alternative positions during labour (walking around as long as possible, squatting, or on hands and knees during the final phase, for example). These are often based on old traditions that favour natural contact between mother and child.

Many maternity hospitals in Sweden have been turned into 'hotels' where the whole family comes to stay in a home-like environment. The forthcoming birth is discussed with the family and arranged according to the family's wishes. The family can often go home after only one day. Post-natal care is taken care of by home visits from a nurse, who comes regularly, for as long as needed. In the case of premature birth the mother is encouraged to stay in hospital with her baby. Instead of using an incubator, the child can be carried by the mother, close to her breast. This method has been used for millennia in South America. It has had very good results both for mother and child, since it encourages good bonding from the very beginning.

The best preparation a woman can have, before she gets pregnant or gives birth, however, is to work through her own negative experiences from birth. Rebirthing is often recommended to pregnant women, as a way to prepare for birth. The more the mother can maintain her openness during birth, the more natural the process will be. After the child is born the mother and child can both benefit from the mother's Rebirthing. A small child is very open to the mother's emotions. The child will show instant changes in behaviour as a response to the mother's feelings. Especially with the first child, a lot of problems are caused by the child's reactions to the mother's stress from the process of adjusting to motherhood. If the mother has a chance to release some of her stress in a Rebirthing session, the child usually responds with much calmer behaviour. The mother can actually have the baby present during Rebirthing sessions. Most children fall asleep, or remain very calm and quiet in this situation.

Many midwives and other staff at maternity hospitals have benefited from Rebirthing. Every time they assist a woman giving birth, it triggers off automatic stress reactions concerning their own birth. By being aware of this phenomenon and by working through their own birth experiences, hospital staff can reduce the stress in their work. They also report that they are much better at giving support to women in labour, and at coping with the situation.

A PSYCHOSOMATIC APPROACH

So far we have been dealing with the physical causes of illness. But to understand how Rebirthing can effectively heal organic disease, a psychosomatic explanation is necessary. This deals with the underlying psychological factors that cause illness. As explained below, Rebirthing's effects in this area can prevent the draining of the body's physical resources and lead to an increase in vitality.

The fact that more and more illnesses are being classified as psychosomatic represents a very significant change in modern medicine. Now, not only are eczema, asthma, menstrual problems, alcoholism and anorexia regarded as such, but also infarct of the heart, high blood pressure and other stress-related illnesses. These diseases are classified as epidemic in USA, according to the latest statistics. Psychomatic illness can be described as a psychological problem which, being ignored, develops into a physical disturbance of the system. It is illness which occurs, or is negatively affected, by stress or other psychological problems. Psychomatic illness arises from a wearing down of the system caused by increased tension in the muscles, raised blood pressure, heartbeat etc.

There is still, however, a difference in attitude towards psychological and physical problems. A psychological problem is perceived as something which can (or even should) be ignored because it is difficult to justify the time, money, or social changes needed to overcome it. Physical illness is seen as more threatening and treatment is often seen as necessary regardless of costs.

> Because of social and cultural conditioning, people often find it impossible to resolve stressful problems in a healthy way and therefore choose – consciously or unconsciously – to get sick as a way out.
>
> *Carl Simonton, interview by Fritjof Capra, 1988*

It is essential to distinguish psychomatic diseases from others. Stress-induced illness can be treated over a lifetime without being cured, unless the underlying causes are dealt with properly. If, on the other hand, the stress that causes a particular disease is recognized and confronted early on, the disease may be cured before it reaches a terminal stage. A great deal of research is being conducted, especially in work-related areas, in an effort to avoid unnecessary stress. More could still be done. Modern medicine could make more use of the holistic approach and adopt a greater flexibility regarding treatment.

> There is a way to take the Pains out of our systems; and we do not need to do surgery to accomplish it. Stored Pain means repressed feeling and disconnected circuits. The solution is feeling and reconnection. Feeling gives us back our unity and organization and makes us come alive in a most literal sense, both physiologically and psychologically. That is surely the way to beat death; the death of our feelings which makes life not worth living, and the death of our bodies which has used up all of its energy in the struggle against Pain.
>
> *Janov, Holden, Primal Man, 1975*

The body has an optimal level of functioning. At this level the body system is balanced enough to provide optimal functioning with minimal effort. The brain's 'pulse', an activity called amplitude, demonstrates the brain's work level. If this level is exceeded, overloading occurs not only in the brain but in all other systems under cerebral control.

Stress is a malfunctioning, a hypermetabolism, created by a raised energy level, body temperature and blood pressure, combined with muscular tension. In some cases, there is also blockage or numbness over whole areas of the body. The heart's work is increased by stress and the pulse accelerates. Though the increase is usually unalarming during routine physical examinations, the system will eventually reach a critical point where the symptoms become manifest. Statistics from regular medical examinations show that there is a general tendency for chronic increases in the test values, such as the heart and pulse rates, in the average population. This points to the fact that widespread stress may be shortening the average lifespan.

An increase in stress will continue as long as experiences too overwhelming for the inner system are blocked and remain in the body. The blocking of memories is not merely a figurative term. It is literally a permanent contraction of the muscles in certain areas of the body. This restricts the body's normal circulation which in turn obstructs the elimination of waste product and the input of 'building materials' for new production of cells. Blocked memories need a certain amount of the body's energy flow to be kept isolated (see Part 3). When we are young the body seems to be able to provide the extra energy needed. But over the years, with an increased number of negative experiences, the energy supply becomes less, as the load to be suppressed increases. This may lead to over-production of hormones, waste of vital energies to maintain hormone levels and muscular tension, blockage of the body's inner flow, pressure on bodily organs, and hindered secretion of bodily fluids. All this wear and tear on the body ages the individual and atrophies all potential energy. In addition to this, another stress effect is caused by the incorrect interpretation of suppressed experiences as a vague longing. This often leads to bad habits, such as overeating, drinking or smoking.

As said earlier, Rebirthing has been shown to have a positive effect on many psychomatic illnesses, especially problems linked with the respiratory system. The relaxation of the respiratory system increases breathing capacity, which in itself has a positive effect. Conscious breathing also lowers the energy level and muscle tension throughout the body, facilitating blood circulation, which is essential for the restoration and healing of previously blocked areas. In addition a second significant transformation occurs in attitude, through the reliving of memories and their subsequent integration. This enhances an individual's insight into his own personality which may cause him or her to seek early treatment for a mental problem before it is expressed in the form of physiological illness.

CANCER

Ideas about the origins of cancer have also been revised in recent years. The connection between emotions and cancer has been observed for several hundred years, but not until recently have several researchers agreed that the inhibition of feelings, mainly anger and grief, and the accumulation of stress can lead to disturbances in the body's immune defence system. In the case of stress, there is evidence that it leads to hormone imbalance. Both conditions, in turn, lead to the production of abnormal cells. Cancer has been described both as 'chaos' or 'despair' on a cellular level.

> One of my main aims, is to reverse the popular image of cancer, which does not correspond to the findings of biological research. Our image of cancer is that of a powerful invader that strikes the body from outside. In reality, the cancer cell is not a powerful cell; it is a weak cell. It does not invade; it pushes out of the way and it is not capable of attacking. Cancer cells are big, but they are sluggish and confused.

> *Carl Simonton, interview by Fritjof Capra, Uncommon Wisdom, 1988*

The fact that the body is inextricably tied to the soul, and hence its illnesses may find their source and their cure in the spirit, has been described by many cancer patients. A woman journalist has given a vivid account of her experience of being diagnosed as having cancer and her struggle to come to terms with her illness and new life situation:

To have cancer is like being pregnant with a monster that has to be aborted – therefore it hurts to get rid of cancer. You cannot, in my view, simply rely on one single school, or alternative medicine to cure you. Everything that helps hurts. It takes a tremendous struggle. I have never before experienced such a connection between body and soul. If you have pain in your soul, you will eventually get all the disharmony that you feel in the soul to be expressed in the cancer. You cannot get rid of cancer without, in some way, also getting straight with your soul.

Damernas Värld, the diary of Barbro Lindström, 1987, translated by the author

The studies of Carl and Stephanie Simonton in America, concerning creative visualization and illness, have revealed several common factors in cancer patients' psychological backgrounds:

Resentment and inability to forget
A tendency toward self pity
Poor ability to develop and maintain meaningful and lasting relationships
Very low self-esteem
A basic denial of life
Loss of a very close friend or relative between six and eighteen months before the diagnosis

In the biological development of cancer, the situation is the opposite of integration; it is fragmentation. For example, the person might think he's not lovable and will carry this fragmented childhood experience through his life as his identity. And then tremendous energy is used to make that identity come true. People often create a whole reality around that fragmented image of themselves.

Carl Simonton, interview by Fritjof Capra, Uncommon Wisdom, 1988

Certain studies have even shown that the characteristics of cancer patients and potential suicides are almost identical. A direct psychological cause of cancer is an inability to integrate negative experiences. From studying drawings by potential cancer patients it is even possible to predict which part of the body will be affected by cancer.

Even high blood pressure, which has been statistically proven to cause cancer, may originate in such fragmented childhood events. Intestinal cancer, which has shown the highest correlation with high blood pressure, affects a part of the body which can store painful memories from the very earliest phase of life. The earliest memories can usually not be reached through the brain since the imprints in the body are made before the brain is developed enough to be affected. The experiences are stored as body memories (expressed as increased tension or malfunction), especially in the inner organs which are developed fully before the brain (see Part 3).

Some of the recent depth therapies have, therefore, sought to deal with both physiological and psychological causes. In a therapy programme conducted by Stanislav Grof in the 1970s, LSD was given to patients in the terminal phase of cancer (Grof, 1977). LSD was originally used because of its opening effect on the body's defence system. In these sessions, many of Grof's patients released traumatic memories derived from various phases of their lives. In connection with their birth, they often displayed strong feelings of 'no way out', and saw their lives as meaningless, devoid of positive opportunities. They described strong energy streaming through their bodies, which dissolved during the drug sessions. For several of the patients the drug sessions meant that their physical condition improved, at least temporarily. Later, Grof replaced the drugs with Holotropic breathing therapy which he developed from his observation of patient's behaviour patterns during the sessions. He focused especially on the changed breathing patterns and the influence of music. The breathing produced similar effects, but without the side-effects of LSD.

BREATHING AND LONGEVITY

The brain was once perceived as an organ which ages irreversibly en route towards death. Aging of the body is currently the subject of diverse opinions among the medical profession. The original theory of the brain's degeneration has been proven incorrect. One recent theory suggests that the brain's interior segments, its oldest parts, begin to age first. Whereas the brain's aging starts from within, the neocortex (the external region) ages very slowly, leaving the thought process relatively untouched even in individuals over 100 years old. The aging of the brain must derive then from our nurture, not our nature. Neurosis, some believe, is the main culprit. The more serious the neurosis, the shorter the lifespan. But both neurosis and aging are not inherent to modern existence. Physical and psychological pain or stress, according to Janov (1975) create a massive restructuring in the brain. This chaos creates a schism between emotion and thought.

> I believe that there is a way to slow the aging process, reduce catastrophic disease which hastens it, and significantly increase our chances of living much longer than we imagined possible. Further, it is my belief that man's longevity has been vastly underestimated. I think that the average human today, even given all the stresses in his environment, should live beyond one hundred years.
>
> *Janov, Holden, Primal Man, 1975*

Leonard Orr has explored the question of the human lifespan more extensively. He has even attempted to discover the path to physical immortality. Based on the idea that the limits of human potential are yet to be divined, he believes that individuals may one day have the ultimate choice of when to die.

Attempts to find the path to physical immortality are not unique to Leonard Orr. It has in fact become one of America's major medical research areas, where vast amounts of money are spent exploring the underlying factors of aging. One of the reasons for the expansion of this research area is the constantly increasing lifespan of the average American. The fact that so many people reach a very advanced age has put a growing strain on medical facilities, threatening a collapse of the whole medical system in America. Researchers hope that finding the key to the aging process will enable old people to be kept healthier for longer, thus reducing their consumption of medical treatment.

The concept of physical immortality is used frequently in Rebirthing, especially in affirmations and other mental techniques (see Part 3) designed to provoke unconscious thoughts about death and the fear of dying.

> Even if death is inevitable, it will not hurt you to believe in physical immortality. It is the safest thought of all. If you are still going to die, the thought of physical immortality will not make any difference. So you can just as well believe in it; it may have the practical implication that it makes you feel well and fantastic while you are alive. When you give up the idea of the inevitability of death, you will experience a tremendous difference.
>
> *Leonard Orr, interview 1989*

The 'death-urge', a person's unconscious longing for death as the ultimate 'way out' of too much pain, is another concept used by Orr. People who incur too many painful experiences may begin to perceive death as an enticing resolution. If too intense, this feeling may leave such an indelible imprint that the person begins to behave in self-destructive ways. When a person gets in contact with his 'death-urge' or re-experiences his unconscious memories of near-death situations, it has a tremendous impact on the psyche and can function as an opening to 'transpersonal experiences' of expanded consciousness (see pages 141–3).

Part 3

THE PSYCHOLOGY OF BREATHING

8

Rebirthing as a Psychotherapeutic Tool

If there is a 'royal way' (to the unconscious) it may consist of deep breathing. Deep breathing techniques, in combination with other methods can, for some patients, contribute to loosing up the immense power of the pain inside the body.

Janov, Primal Scream, 1970

Rebirthing is not in itself psychotherapy, but like other breathing methods it is used as a psychotherapeutic tool. Rebirthing acts as a cleansing process for the body and psyche causing everything which blocks the body's natural flow to emerge. This emergence makes it possible for the obstructions to be integrated and dissolved. Because of this, it is not only important for the individual's therapist to be competent enough to guide breathing, but he or she also needs to be able to create an environment of trust and confidence, and to be qualified to handle the level of psychological problems that can emerge during this process.

A Personal Example

During my first few breathing sessions it was very difficult for me to lie still when I was breathing. As soon as I entered the energy cycle, my head began to turn from side to side. Giving into the slightest impulse to move resulted in an immediate desire to kick as hard as I could. Because of these temptations I was, on one occasion, encouraged to simply pursue the feelings and forget the breathing altogether. Consequently I began to kick and roll around the floor like a mad kick-boxer. Five or six people assisted me. *Armed with cushions and mattresses, they surrounded me and pressed against me in order to provide a 'resistance' against which to struggle. But they were unable to hold me; I broke through their wall of pillows and hurtled across the room until I hit the wall. I was possessed by an overwhelming rage, the existence of which I had never suspected.*

Such wild reactions continued to be an element of my breathing sessions until one session, in which I finally encountered a strong sense of liberation. A steel band, which had been holding back some part of my being, seemed to suddenly burst. Henceforth, my breathing sessions became much calmer and more centred around experiences of energy and general well being.

It should be said here that there may be great differences between the structure of various Rebirthing sessions. Some therapists work with a combination of breathing and other exercises, such as the interventionist approach mentioned above, body harmony or visualization. This combination of therapies is aimed at facilitating access to subconscious memories. This is not to say that Rebirthing necessarily benefits from being combined with other therapies, but simply that various approaches can be appropriate at different times and with different people. The essential factor in all these approaches is that they aim at triggering the spontaneous energy cycle – 'the healing of the breath'. This means that there may be an active role for the therapist at the beginning of the session, but for as long as the energy cycle lasts there is no need for any interference with the breathing.

The first breathing sessions are usually dominated by memories stored closest to the surface, in the subconscious. Although a person may feel submerged in emotions and memories, the entire scene occurs while one is awake and conscious of the process. Rebirthing is, in a sense, like dreaming while being completely awake. As in dreams the person is simultaneously the actor and audience of his own play. Unlike hypnosis or drug therapy, a Rebirthing session always depends on the person's readiness to be open. Thus, the experience can only reach the depths that the person allows. Though the same experiences may have to be integrated gradually over a number of sessions, it will lead to contact with deeper, more painful recollections. Often it ends in memories of childhood, birth or even the time in the womb. Once the most traumatic events of a person's life have been worked through and integrated, the breathing sessions become mainly calm and undramatic. They evolve into a kind of meditation, revitalizing or re-energizing the self.

> The most important result of the practice of 'anapana-sati' or 'mindfulness with regard to breathing', is the realization that the process of breathing is the connecting link between conscious and subconscious, gross-material and fine-material, volitional and non-volitional functions, and therefore the most perfect expression of the nature of all life.
>
> *Govinda, Foundations of Tibetan Mysticism, 1960*

THE BODY'S DEFENCE MECHANISM

Rebirthing works as a psychotherapeutic tool through its inherent integration of blocked memories, which acts as a psychic cleansing process. In order to understand this process, it is essential to first know how the body's psychic defence operates.

In a healthy person the brain and body function in unison. One thinks what one feels and vice versa. Within the brain itself there is harmony; both the left and the right half of the brain interact in all processes. When the body's basic needs are left unfulfilled it is experienced as pain or stress (both psychological or physical) in the organism. The experience of pain or stress is as vital as hunger and sleep. Stress is simply the body's signal to restore homeostasis, like shivering when cold or sweating when warm. Stress can be sparked by lack of food, proper care, loving contact and/or other needs essential for survival and development, especially during the first years of our lives. Animals deprived of their mothers have shown in several studies that lack of love and care can cause significant damage to the system. Tests with monkeys have shown that even an ugly-looking doll made of wires and a towel will be accepted by a baby monkey as a compensatory mother. Similar effects of maternal deprivation have also been sadly illustrated in the recent reports of Romanian orphans.

Because too much stress can provoke catastrophic consequences, the body has developed a sophisticated defence mechanism against it. From the first splitting of cells, the organism develops a system aimed at maintaining inner balance. The primary way to defend the body against pain is to become unaware of it. For physical pain this entails becoming unconscious when the pain gets too much. For psychological pain, the gate level that controls the inflow to consciousness is altered so that we are kept unaware of reality. This gate mechanism works in two ways. Outer reality is adjusted to inner truth and vice versa. Anything perceived as negative and damaging to the inner system is blocked before it reaches consciousness. We stop experiencing consciously what is too painful for our integrity. We cannot be aware of more than the body or psyche will find acceptable. Too much threat to our person may cause an overload of consciousness and a total collapse of the body. A person can die of shock.

Thoughts that are too discomforting are transferred to the subconscious. They are stored by the right side of the brain. This side of the brain has no sense of time, which means that everything stored this way is maintained in its exact form for any length of time, often throughout a person's life. Being stored in the subconscious also means a loss of contact with the original pain. This, however, does not mean that it stops having an effect on behaviour, it merely ceases to have a direct meaning. Many people have a vague sense of a hidden force in themselves which is beyond their command. This is caused by the tendency of the subconscious to have a stronger impact than ordinary thought because it is out of reach of the control of conscious will. Once the subconscious thought is revealed, the reaction is often: 'Is that all there is to it?'. The first event that was blocked may have caused a reaction – like a stone dropped into water – of a wave of feelings. Because the memory's origin is unknown, it may acquire a gradually growing importance, since the imagination has a tendency to bias perception, especially when there is an element of stress involved. This may often have a negative effect in the sense that a psychological disturbance which has great impact on the adult person's life may be caused by a small incident that has grown over the years. One example of this is phobias. For instance, fear of heights, which may be traced back to an unpleasant feeling of 'being dropped' out of the womb due to careless handling as a newborn.

THE ORIGIN OF THE DEFENCE SYSTEM

The formation of the body's defence system is one of the earliest phases of human development. The main need of early human beings (hominids) was the ability to mobilize all their resources in order to survive attacks from animals or other human beings. Rational clear thinking was more important than emotional experience. To avoid immediate danger, alertness was needed for a short period of time, but to the maximum extent, regardless of strain on the body. The threat being gone, the body could again rest and replenish its resources.

The caveman's brain needed to be alert, and not overwhelmed, in dangerous situations, and to be able to make the right decisions in order to survive. A main function of the defence mechanism was to adjust impressions from the outer world to an acceptable inner level. Ideally, they should be kept at a level that would allow the body to function optimally at all times. If outer impressions were allowed to reach the brain at full intensity the individual might incur paralysis or die from the shock of the situation. A system thus developed that bypasses consciousness, sending information directly out to various parts of the body as simple reflexes. This 'short-cut' reflex also manifests itself physically when, for example, a person pulls his fingers away from a hot stove before being aware that the hand is being burnt.

Every species has formed its own unique pattern for survival. For the human being this is the brain's adeptness at deducing new behaviours from previous experiences. The brain works almost as a video camera, capturing and registering all the details of a whole event in order to 'replay' them in safety. When all the knowledge is integrated into the body, the memory itself is unnecessary and is therefore dissolved.

The way we observe the world around us does not give us an objective picture. The eyes register and send on signals that are interpreted and processed by the brain to form a picture. What a person experiences as an 'objective image', is a deduction or construction from the brain. This process involves both sides of the brain. The picture is created by logical, rational deductions based on external information registered by the senses in combination with emotional and sensory reactions to this information. This process occurs mainly in the left side of the brain, but is based on information from previous experience stored in the right side. These pictures eventually add to the stored knowledge (wisdom) in the right side of the brain.

It is essential to bear in mind that the continual aim of this defence mechanism is the maintenance of rational behaviour. Each rational decision will be based both on the present situation and on conscious and subconscious memories from previous comparable situations. Consciousness, however, will only be cognizant of the conscious information. Previous subconscious memories will be unavailable. Hence, the rationality in our conduct is often difficult to detect, when parts of the underlying information are out of reach of our conscious mind. Behaviour is thus often incorrectly seen as irrational and out of context, when the real problem is being out of synchronization. That is to say that the behaviour is rational but not necessarily as regards the present situation. Reactions can be based on both past and present experiences, with only the present situation available for our conscious understanding.

THE SYMPATHETIC–PARASYMPATHETIC SYSTEM

For the body to function optimally at all times, it must have two distinct 'work levels' in the autonomic nervous system. It has therefore developed one sympathetic and one parasympathetic function: the former alerts the body to stress signals, the latter relaxes the body when the signals indicate 'end of danger'. A healthy person maintains a balance between these systems.

To elaborate, the sympathetic system sounds the alarm bell and provides an aggressive, energy-consuming reaction. The body is mobilized, the pulse and blood pressure raised, urine and stress hormones are dispersed. These interior reactions lead to impulsive, extroverted action in which the muscles contract and the breathing is shallow, with short breaths high in the chest. All impressions are thus prohibited from reaching too profoundly into the body in order to maximize the body's physical force.

The parasympathetic system contributes, on the other hand, a passive, immobile, energy-saving reaction. It thereby calms the body's vital functions, makes the muscles relax, lowers the voice and slows movement (as in a state of sleep or deep relaxation). Since the tension of the muscles is lowered, breathing becomes deeper and more open. The body opens up, facilitating circulation. This is also a signal for the brain to start the 'replay mechanism' for processing and integrating impressions.

THE DEVELOPMENT OF THE DEFENCE SYSTEM

Because the brain is the nexus of human survival it must be protected from the very beginning of life. Although a newborn baby has no language to express its thoughts, the central areas of its body and brain are sufficiently developed to commence blocking and storing memories. At this stage, these are 'body memories' which means that they are recollections of bodily reactions (e.g. the discomfort of hunger, the pleasure of a soft breast full of delicious milk). Particular regions of the brain take several years to develop fully, but the gate mechanisms for protection against too painful stimuli begin to develop from the very beginning, alongside the various bodily functions. The more the child develops and can survive on its own, the less the protection of the brain is needed. The child learns to control its body and distinguish danger in its environment. Therefore the gate mechanism alters in accordance with the level of bodily development. Janov (1975) divides these levels into three main groups:

The Bodily Functions

The first stress experienced by the foetus concerns bodily needs. Because the brain is not yet fully developed, it is less able to integrate impressions. This results in the deepest, internal inhibitions. Being incapable, at this age, of discriminating between various unsatisfied needs, they must all be seen as potentially life threatening. As an extra safety measure, the newborn baby has a lower threshold against pain, and reacts with greater rapidity to block it than, for example, a ten-year-old. The infant reacts to all kinds painful experiences with constant crying, colic, sleep or evasive movements of the body. Though the body absorbs the pain, it does not mean that it is automatically dissolved. The pain remains in the various regions until properly integrated, causing increased stress which can lead to future illness in the stomach, colon and other central organs.

The Emotional Functions

By the age of three, the child has access to language and the brain is developed enough to give an emotional context to any painful experience. The mental image of being left too long as a newborn can now be verbally expressed and interpreted as 'my parents do not care about me'. Reactions at this level are therefore often outbursts of anger and other extreme emotions.

The Cognitive Functions

The brain, by the age of six, is sufficiently formed to distinguish between a multitude of feelings and to comprehend them to a certain extent. The child can make coherent connections between experiences. Therefore, such forms of blocking, as rationalization and misinterpretation, begin to ensue in areas of the brain which concern consciousness. Experiences which are still too painful are blocked. For example, the recollection of not having enough attention from the parents is given an outlet in symbolic substitutes. This can mean adopting behaviour that the parents are sure to appreciate. These rationalizations can also be internalized to such an extent that the person is convinced the symbolic world is, in fact, the real world. The person adopts the exact opposite view: that the parents were capable of showing deep care for their child and that the childhood was happy. Such a person will exist symbolically in their head, shut off at all levels, instead of having contact with their feelings and bodily needs.

INTEGRATION

The body's defence mechanism had a clear purpose and a perfect design when stress was caused by distinct outer experiences. Then there was a clear initiator – a wild animal appearing on the scene – and a clear end – returning to safety in the cave. The brain does not, however, have the ability to distinguish between real physical danger and contrived psychological danger. Though the reactions themselves are the same, as soon as there is any cause for alert, the brain does not notice that the danger is part of a created picture without correspondence to the outer world. Given the ability to reflect on itself and its creative capacity, however, (as occurs in conscious breathing or meditation) the brain can acquire the capacity to distinguish the psychological stress and deal with it in a calmer way.

Most stress today is a continual psychological stress lacking a distinct beginning or end. Though the actual problems are of an abstract nature, like work, money, or relationships, the body copes with these secondary dangers in the same way as with real threats to life. 'A safe place' is still necessary for integrating impressions, because only if that process is completed will the body release the relevant memories from the subconscious. The brain's enormous capacity to store information is both beneficial and detrimental because when memories need to be repressed, it requires the body's energy to keep them down.

The sympathetic-parasympathetic reactions normally act upon signs of stress or relaxation in the body. Given the right circumstances, such as being safely asleep in bed, the process can start spontaneously. But it can also be initiated at will. A person may do so by lying down in a secure environment, relaxing the body and the breathing to a certain level, all of which will give the right signals to the body to start the integration process.

When feelings are hindered to prevent 'overloading' of the inner system, they are 'frozen' and encapsulated somewhere within the body. They remain in the exact form and strength as they were initially perceived, being stored in a way that is not affected by time or other external circumstances. The chemical makeup, of which a particular 'memory' consists, gets stuck where it first acted upon the body.

The integration of incoming impressions occurs when the tension in the muscles is released and the chemical 'memory' can pass into the fluids of the body. That is also to say that incoming information is finally let into consciousness. Only then can blocked responses be fully experienced. In order for the gate mechanism to allow this, the circumstances must be perceived as acceptable to the organism. As said earlier, the threshold values against pain are lowest at the earliest phases of life, for the maximum protection of the organism, before the child can survive on its own and has learned to distinguish threats to the body. This is why so many experiences are blocked during this period. This means, on the other hand, that when an adult person releases blocked memories, they may easily pass through the gate to consciousness, since they are well within the adult's level of acceptance.

Memories have to be re-experienced at the level where they were blocked in order to be fully integrated. In other words, it is not possible to remember very early experiences except through bodily memories, since they were blocked before the brain was developed enough to be involved in the process. Such experiences therefore have not left a clear imprint in the brain. These memories cannot be reached through the mind alone, but have to be approached through relaxation and openness in the body. Otherwise it is impossible to reach into the parts of the body where the memories are actually stored.

It is a matter of the depth of realization of it. You can relive it all endlessly and never get it out of the system. There are two routes, two pathways, to get to it; regression, going backwards in time to it, or there is recession, going back in the mind to a place beyond distinctions and differentiations, a meditative depth.

R.D. Laing, interview, N. Albery, *How to Feel Reborn*, 1985

Most depth psychotherapies have their special ways to express and relive stored emotions and memories. A common factor is to increase the openness of the body through the expression of emotions. In Rebirthing, however, the focus is placed upon the actual energy release that occurs when emotions are released and expressed. Whether the emotion is expressed through screaming, crying, talking or body movements, there is a point in time when the expression of a feeling has a healing effect. This occurs when the expressed emotion has caused an opening in the body large enough to allow a release of energy. At this point the body will actually 'let go' of the stored feeling and allow integration. Then the actual healing of the body takes place.

There are various methods of reaching this point, but acting out the feeling is not a necessary ingredient. The essential opening can be attained by focusing on the energy release in the breathing. Any emotion can, in fact, be expressed merely as 'energy in the breathing'. The important part is not the outer expression but the opening of the body and the releasing of withheld energy.

This is how Rebirthing has become such an effective tool for integration and a real key to the subconscious. Often only a minor change in the outer situation is required to allow for the release of even the most painful memories. By creating the right circumstances through relaxed breathing in a safe environment, it is possible to reach the very deep relaxation that is the perfect condition for the body system to open up to the integration process.

A Rebirthing session can, in a way, be described as an intensified, conscious dream period. Dreams occur when the conscious part of the brain is at rest. Though dreams are important 'processors' of information gathered during the day, they are not sufficient to cope with constant stress, nor will they provide much understanding of the subconscious, unless they are worked with in some kind of dream therapy. The conditions of a Rebirthing session are much the same as the dream state: the body is relaxed, lying down; maintaining the breathing involves very little effort; the increase of oxygen gives the body much energy. These factors together create a perfect situation for the release and integration of stored memories. Experience has shown that once the main part of the integration process is finished, the mind is able to expand into other realms, as is also seen in meditation. This aspect of conscious breathing may lead to experiences often described as 'transpersonal' (see Part 4).

During conscious breathing sessions it is also possible to detect the age at which the blocking occurred by seeing what form of expression it takes. A person who reacts to stress with problems in the stomach or colon, for example, is most likely to have blocked occurrences from very early stages of bodily development. Facial grimaces or emotional outbursts are most likely to be traced to blocking at the age of emotional development. A person who reacts with the intellect, however, has sustained this blocking from a later phase of maturation. A person who reacts with the intellect can, however, also have blocking at other levels. The dissolution of blocking at the cognitive level can lead to emotional reactions instead, whose dissolution in turn can open the way for bodily reactions related to the same source.

When the body is fully developed the various stages of development overlap. Blocked memories from the time around birth and early childhood affect the threshold values for reactions in the other ages. This means that when blocked memories are integrated, they start with the most recent experiences, reaching back in time, until contact is made with blocking which occurred near birth. This is due to the effect of the gate mechanism which maintains the gradation of the blocked memories in accordance with the threshold level when they were blocked. This may mean that a harmless experience of strong light at birth may be regarded as more of a 'threat' to the system than a car accident for the adult, since the first experience was blocked when the threshold level was much lower.

Integration in the body makes the memories and emotions lose their indirect, subconscious influence over behaviour. Instead they are added to the ordinary 'memory bank', referred to as our wisdom or knowledge. Integration will also mean an increase in physical energy, stemming from the release of blocked energy and relaxation in the body, due to the muscles no longer needing to maintain their tension. At the same time, the circulation of the body fluids will be freer and more balanced. On the mental level, an increased feeling of wholeness and balance is felt and fewer parts of the personality are subconscious and thereby inexplicable. Behaviour becomes more rational, and judgements more objective, reacting only to present situations. In all, this leads to an increased openness and expanded self-confidence.

It is recommended, especially when just starting to practise Rebirthing, to allow enough time between the breathing sessions to let the body and psyche adjust and integrate what has been experienced. The average energy cycle, completed without disturbances during a breathing session, takes 1 to 2 days to integrate fully. Sometimes, however, the breathing session can cause a delayed reaction, in which nothing occurs at the time. It is not until after the session that the emotions and memories emerge, often triggered by some incident in everyday life. Also, if the energy cycle has been disrupted, or is too disturbed by a memory reaction, it may have to be completed at a later date. This can be done any time during the same session, or in a new session shortly thereafter.

BIRTH TRAUMA

The name Rebirthing arose during the first development of the technique, when it was found that many of the released memories dealt with the individual's birth. The integration and subsequent dissolution of the birth trauma actually affected a 'rebirth' of the personality, emancipating both body and mind. Individuals experienced a transformation not only in their opinions and perceptions, but also in their behavioral patterns, self-esteem and world view. The preliminary explanation for this suggested that the cause lay solely in the re-experiencing of the birth trauma itself. But recent interpretations have been more expansive, suggesting that the real importance of re-experiencing the birth trauma is due to the fact that it is often the first memory to be blocked, in a chain of blocked memories linked with a specific feeling or experience. This first memory leads to a predisposition of the brain to block all other similar experiences (as a sort of safety measure to ensure that anything linked with the first memory will not be experienced by the inner system) (see COEX-system on pages 114–15).

The first years of Rebirthing witnessed a great emphasis on birth experiences including, quite frequently the French physician Leboyer's description of the good birth. Chapters of his book *Birth Without Violence* were read aloud and films displaying birth situations were shown before the breathing sessions to facilitate contact with birth memories. As a pioneer of a new attitude toward childbirth, his ideas were greatly appreciated. By focusing on birth from the infant's perspective, he was one of the first to show that a newborn's screams and writhing face were not inherent to birth. His photographs, taken in a calm, relaxed atmosphere with maximum adjustment to the child's needs, showed relaxed and smiling children. His theories departed from what had generally been believed before, and made way for a greater understanding of the child's experience. Not too long ago, knowledge of newborn children was so lacking that people assumed them to be completely insensitive. Operations were even performed on babies without anesthetics. Some claimed that the child did not experience any emotions during its first years. The medical research in maternity hospitals dealt largely with the well-being of the mother and the medical staff instead of the infant. Fortunately, a shift in emphasis has occurred. In many hospitals, research is aimed at finding methods of assistance which promote natural labour and are good for both mother and child.

Although a normal birth is in itself a dramatic and powerful experience, the child is prepared for it by nature. It does not have to be a traumatic event. At a natural birth both mother and child are 'pre-programmed' to work together to make the birth as smooth as possible. This 'programming' concerns the flow of hormones which manipulates the stages of birth. The same principle applies to hormone changes during the menstruation cycle. However, in the case of pregnancies, the hormone flow from the mother triggers the appropriate reactions in the child, which in turn triggers the next reaction in the mother. If no interference occurs during this process, the birth will take place according to 'nature's plan', without complications or trauma.

If the child and mother are handled with care, blocked traumatic memories will not necessarily develop (in either the child or the parents). Handling with care may mean the reduction of disturbing effects in the environment (strong noise or light, extremes of temperature), or allowing the baby to stay with the mother until it has recovered and adjusted to the new environment. Another important factor is that the baby is allowed sufficient time to start breathing on its own, before the umbilical cord is cut. This gives the lungs a chance to gradually move and expand as they are brought into use. The period immediately following birth has proved to be the most important time for mother and child to bond (as well as assisting the father–child bond).

The various phases of birth are inherent in the child's 'programming' and are in themselves no cause for alarm. If the birth is allowed to follow its instinctual course and time period, every aspect of it can be experienced as basically positive. Although birth may be physically painful for the mother, this positive feeling will reverberate through to the child. Experiences can then be handled internally without the need to block threatening stimuli. Studies of adults have shown that this type of positive birth experience has a very positive impact on the future adult's self-confidence, trust and ability to cope with trying situations.

Unfortunately, normal birth is not as common as nature would have it. This is not necessarily caused by the lack of a safe environment or medical care, but more commonly by the people who are present. Furthermore, although everything may initially indicate a normal birth, complications can occur at any time during labour, caused by the disturbing effects of the mother's birth memories. They may affect her behaviour, thereby causing a change in the baby's reaction. A natural labour is a 'fine-tuned instrument', which requires openness in the mother. It is very difficult for a mother to give birth to her child without being influenced by her own birth memories. Just being in the environment of the hospital or experiencing the birth hormone flow can trigger her own memories. Even if the mother is oblivious to them, her body will react by blocking discomforting memories. The natural process is thereby shut off.

Even if the mother maintains her openness throughout the birth, the father, or staff present, can cause disruptions. If the members of the staff grow anxious because of their own unconscious birth trauma, they may unknowingly misjudge what is taking place due to their own fears. Also, this intense disquiet or stress may also radiate through to the mother and child, who are exceptionally adept at interpreting body signals. For the unborn child, in particular, these signals are the main source of information about the world inside and outside the womb. The best support that the child can receive during the gestation period is thus a calm, loving environment. Calm people, detached from their own feelings and able to stay focused on the present situation regardless of what happens, will radiate positive feelings to the child. There is no better way in which we can transmit to the child the information that the apparently life-threatening situation is under control.

Although much has improved in recent years, birth is still, for many people, the most dangerous and traumatic event in their lives. When a child is born it does not yet have the experience to judge the situation accurately and to be adequately sensitive to what is happening. Before enough experience is accumulated, the defence mechanism is designed to treat every situation as a potential danger to the organism. Each incident is met with a total alertness of the senses and every threat is blocked from reaching the vital inner parts. All the impressions hit the child with full force which means that even the slightest disturbance, such as a bright light, loud noise or harsh handling, is perceived as threatening.

In many cases birth is literally a struggle for life. Perhaps the womb may not open even when the child signals it is ready to be born. Or the passage through the birth channel may not be elastic enough for the child to pass. The umbilical cord may have a strangulating effect with the child being incorrectly positioned inside the womb, unable to come out head first.

The most common complications at birth are part of everyday routine for hospitals, and usually not life threatening for the child. Some examples are:

the child is born too soon/late

the contractions of labour are too slow/fast

the mother receives a local anesthetic or other drugs which affect the child

the child has to be delivered by cesarian or suction apparatus

the child is separated too soon from the mother

too strong impressions from the environment, such as bright light, loud noise and insensitive hands

the umbilical cord is cut too soon

BIRTH MEMORIES

All too often, the ideal birth situation is not achieved and the child is forced to rely on its own resources in such a difficult and dangerous situation. The birth situation can be similar to having a severe accident in a remote place where, regardless of mental anxiety and physical exhaustion, the person must save himself. Even if the person were a physician with special training in wildlife survival and a strong religious faith, this experience would inevitably leave a traumatic scar.

To the inexperienced child the birth situation means that it must mobilize all its resources. The imprint this has on the child acts like a severe shock in the nervous system and the brain, and may lead to life-long tensions throughout the system. The blocking of impressions can lead to a continuous mobilization of directly measurable energy tied up in the brain and body.

Traditional psychotherapy has emphasized the psychological trauma on the child. Rebirthing and other depth therapies have shown, on the other hand, that as far as perinatal memories are concerned, it is the physical traumas which have a larger impact on the psyche. A physically difficult birth, severe illness, accident or operation is a greater threat to the psyche than the fact that the child was separated from the mother during the event.

These depth therapies have shown, further, that it is quite possible to re-experience such an incidence. When birth experiences or traumatic physical experiences are revitalized in a breathing session, they sometimes cause dramatic bodily reactions ranging from acute shortness of breath to sharp pains in various areas of the body, or paralysis. Bruises and other marks on the body may also appear. In some cases it has been verified that the bruises are actual replicas of the marks from the original trauma. The symptoms and marks usually remain until shortly after the breathing session but may, in some cases, be visible for a longer period of time. The same reactions may occur over a span of breathing sessions until the entire experience is integrated.

If the birth was very painful physically, the memories may appear as constant reminders in the form of malfunctions of certain organs or systems. A common memory that many people suffer from is restriction of the breath. If the umbilical cord was cut too soon, before the lungs were able to gradually expand, the first breath can be very painful. When the umbilical cord, the original lifeline through which all 'breathing' occurs, is severed, the little child experiences a sense of suffocation, which is very traumatic. In order to survive, it must take a breath, but often the panicking child feels forced to use the lungs too rapidly and too fully. Breathing will therefore probably always be linked with the experience of pain and of near-death. The memory of this first breath may lead to a life-long tightening of the respiratory muscles. Unless this memory is released, it will always prohibit the breathing from being fully relaxed.

Janov (1982) gives many examples of the enduring reactions in the nervous system propagated by various types of birth. A long birth, he says, often leads to a sympathetic system reaction within the child. If, because of her own trauma, the mother is either unattuned to the hormone signals from her child, or too rigid to open up, the child will find its passage through the birth channel strenuous and long. The parasympathetic reaction is often linked with a near-death experience, such as breech birth, a strangling umbilical cord or an overly-sedated mother drugged during labour. The child may have needed stimulation to initiate the breathing and body functions. The parasympathetic reaction occurs on a low energy level and produces a child who is often calm, undemanding, passive and seldom cries. This child is often appreciated by the parents and other adults, since few realize that the 'good behaviour' can be caused by the birth trauma which still has an overwhelming impact and pacifying effect on the child. As an adult the parasympathetic person is often careful, passive, pessimistic, conservative and has low self-esteem. This person often worries about the future without realizing that this is caused by memories of the past.

The memory of a birth trauma is often expressed later in behavioral patterns which reflect the birth: a tendency to always be late or early, to avoid getting to bed at night or getting out of bed in the morning, to delay decisions or the inability to make decisions. To such people, simple everyday incidents as, for instance, a traffic jam, may force them to risk their lives, as well as those of others, in dangerous driving in order to free themselves from the feeling of being stuck. Excessive noise, loud music or complete quietude may even cause them stress. Unfortunately, such conduct is often excused as being part of the individual's personality and is rarely linked with its probable origin.

Grof (1988) also gives many examples of the various effects of birth on adult behaviour. A child delivered with manual aid by forceps often tends to be enthusiastic initially in everyday situations, but later depends on others for the completion phase. A child brought forth under the influence of anesthetics may experience complications in mobilizing the energy to begin new projects in life and often loses the sense of focus in their enterprises. If a birth is induced, the adult person may dislike being 'pushed into situations' prematurely. Patterns related to caesarean births may actually be divided into planned operations and emergency operations. The planned operation is significant because the whole phase of struggling to leave the womb is bypassed, leaving a fairly untraumatic birth memory. In the case of an emergency operation the child has experienced an intense struggle against death and is often left with a more shocking memory than average, and will tend to overreact inexplicably in certain situations.

In a secondary phase birth memories can conceivably lead to asthma, a constant cough, a pressure in the head or shoulders, knots in the stomach, heart palpitations, chronic exhaustion, dizziness and nausea. The premenstrual syndrome may also be linked to cyclical hormone changes stimulated by birth memories; the heightened anxiety, irritability, depression and anger, etc, are all symptoms reminiscent of the emotional spectrum encountered at birth.

A Personal Experience

My adulthood has been plagued with stomach problems which occur during stressful periods of my everyday life. Whether I am simply nervous before doing something, or someone speaks or acts negatively towards me, I literally feel pain in my stomach.

During my breathing sessions, I have often had images and experiences in which my stomach is a big, open hole within me. My reaction has been to spontaneously protect my stomach, rolling up into a foetal position, placing pillows against my stomach to protect myself from the feeling of being vulnerable in this area.

In the course of such a breathing session I was guided by my therapist into mentally reliving my childhood. I returned to the time before my birth and experienced myself as a foetus, linked with my mother through the umbilical cord. At the same time I felt waves of anger and frustration crashing like tidal waves through the umbilical chord into my stomach, each one very painful.

My initial reaction was to recede into a state resembling sleep. When the therapist asked me about my experiences, I could only repeat: 'I don't know, I don't want to know, I don't want to feel'. Despite this avoidance, she continued to insist on an answer. Still my only reaction was that of clinging to unconsciousness of the occurrence. When we later discussed this experience, I realized suddenly how often I handle unpleasant situations by making my mind insensitive and distant.

PERSONAL LAWS

The sympathetic-parasympathetic system determines how we react, act and create our personalities. It has an extraordinary influence on human attitudes, from the most intricate emotions, values and ideas to the simplest body posture and sexuality. The way we reacted to our first experiences in life becomes a pattern for everything that occurs later in life. Although the child is unable to make a rational, intellectual interpretation of the situation, the experience will lead to a body memory that will affect all future impressions, colouring the subconscious 'conclusions' and forming the base for firm ideas about the world. Being, so to say, based on 'pre-brain memories' that exist in the body, but not the mind, it is very difficult to establish their origin. These ideas are so rooted that they are usually considered to be our intrinsic character. In Rebirthing terminology they are known as 'personal laws'.

A strenuous struggle to be born forms the basis of many such 'personal laws'. A symptomatic reaction might be 'I have to struggle hard to get where/what I want', or 'Nobody is there to help me when I need them'. Whatever these vague memories reflect will later on in life be formed gradually into very strong beliefs. The memories will be there colouring the perception of every following event. Without anyone having taught the child, it gradually 'draws the conclusion' derived from the first experience of the birth situation, that life is hard and rough. This child will probably grow up to become a person with an aggressive temperament, sympathetic system reactions to stress and generally a high energy level. From a social perspective these are not negative qualities (many successful businessmen and women have this temperament), but it can lead to an excessively high level of energy, and it can be difficult for the body to get the rest and relaxation that it needs. It also has a distorting effect on perception obstructing objectivity and the ability to focus on the present.

The personal laws can be divided into five major areas, based on the most common experiences reported from Rebirthing sessions. They are:

1 Birth trauma
2 Parental disapproval
3 Specific negatives
4 Unconscious death-urge
5 Other lifetimes

Extremely distressing births can lead to more serious neurotic disturbances. The effects of birth trauma, according to Grof (1988), may range from simple problems to addictions or compulsive behaviour, to severe mental illness such as manic depression and schizophrenia. Phobias, seen in this perspective, are reactions which are a mixture of emotions and intellect, with the stress on emotions. Fanaticism is a similar disturbance which, on the other hand, affects the intellect. Claustrophobia, fear of heights and dizziness are often linked with being 'trapped' during birth or being held without proper support immediately after birth. Fear of the dark and claustrophobia can also be related to the time in the womb. Another type of phobia, the 'counter phobia', where there is a compulsion to constantly prove one's bravery, can be linked with birth trauma. In this case, the fear itself is so great that every sign of it, later in life, has to be avoided, since it may trigger threatening memories. This often leads to a compulsion to engage in life-threatening activities, thereby giving the person a chance to prove himself to be extremely fearless, or able to control his fear. Sexual disturbances may reveal incorrect signals from the hypothalamus caused by blocked experiences, or they may be a way of dissolving strong inner tensions. The orgasm and epileptic seizures are various ways for the body to let out spasms that can dissolve tensions. Such easing of tensions are, however, only temporary.

As stated above, the physical and psychological state of the mother has a great influence on the foetus. Many so-called inherited qualities can be seen as imprints made when the mother's thoughts and feelings are 'chemically' transferred into the foetus. Her own experiences are transferred to the child, along with her interpretations. This covert influence is carried on throughout life with its most obvious significance in the earliest phase of life, before the child has incurred its own experiences, constructs and learnt social behaviour.

The mother's feelings and experiences during pregnancy also form the framework for her upcoming relationship with the child. Most parents are familiar with the phrase, 'It's not what you teach the child that will have effect, but what you do'. The mother's unconscious idea about a certain matter will have a greater impact on the child than what she consciously thinks or says about it. Regardless of parents' good intentions, the child will learn both overt and covert behaviour from them. In the process, the child may also perceive that a parent's words do not always correspond with body language and the telepathic message transmitted. Although human beings focus on verbal and open interaction, we are still sensitive to each other's thoughts and able to read the subconscious messages revealed in body language and small changes in appearance. The young child who has not yet developed language, is especially sensitive to these signals. But the mother of a young child also attunes herself to the child's signals before the child can communicate directly with language. Most mothers learn to distinguish between subtle signals from her child and to sense the baby's needs even when they are separated. For example, a mother often awakens just before the child starts crying to signal it needs attention.

Recent years have seen several studies of this transmission of emotions. It has been found that children, in particular, are sensitive to unspoken emotions, especially in their parents. The children do not simply notice the emotions, but often also act them out. When a mother, despite her controlled appearance, is very upset inside, she can cause an apparently inexplicable tantrum in her child. She transmits her covert feelings to the child, who has not yet achieved the same restrictions upon his or her feelings.

Another illustration of the transmission of thoughts is shown in a study of the effect of parent's expectations upon their child's performance (Russell, 1984). Ninety per cent of the children whose parents believed they performed below average showed signs of psychological disturbance by the age of ten, while children whose parents believed in their ability showed disturbance only in 50 per cent of the cases.

Perhaps the greatest problem in curbing the effects of this transmission is that most parents are unaware that it is even occurring, or what thoughts and feelings they themselves are experiencing. Parental upbringing of a child is primarily based on good conscious intentions. But the subconscious emotional ('gut-level') reaction stemming from the parent's own childhood also inevitably has an effect. These emotions must be rediscovered and re-experienced before they can be understood. Until they are integrated, the parent will not be able to completely separate his or her own childhood experiences from those of the child. This may lead to the unwanted repetition of their own child-parent relationship and so on, over several generations.

THE COEX SYSTEM

When a person has integrated a sufficient amount of his blocked memories, a dominant 'theme' or 'key memory' that affects and colours all other memories becomes discernible. In Rebirthing they are known as 'personal laws'. Stanislav Grof has categorized these memories in what he calls a COEX system. He defines the COEX system as 'a dynamic constellation of memories (and associated fantasy material), from different periods of the individual's life, with the common denominator of a strong emotional charge of the same quality, intense physical sensations of the same kind, or the fact that they share some other important elements'. (Grof, 1985, page 97) The deepest layers in the system are experiences from the foetal period and the time around birth. The surface memories are similar experiences from later periods in life. A COEX system may, for example, contain memories of each time a person has been humiliated, or of each experience of fear or anxiety.

The most important part of the COEX system is the key experience. The key experience is the first of a special kind of prototypic incident which is registered in the brain. It forms the foundation of a specific

COEX system and becomes a prototype that will have a great influence and colouring on the registering of later experiences of the same kind. Grof has divided the key experiences in the COEX system according to his BPM (Birth Perinatal Matrices) into four different categories.

1 The first stage. Experiences in the womb before labour have started. The original bonding with the mother. The spiritual equivalent is a soul union with the universe.

2 The second stage. Contractions in a closed womb system. Antagonism against the mother. The spiritual commensurate is hell.

3 The third stage. The passage out through the birth canal. Cooperation with the mother. The spiritual equivalent is death-rebirth.

4 The fourth stage. The termination of the symbiotic union and the forming of a new relationship. The separation from the mother. Spiritual comparison is the death of the ego and rebirth.

The strong emotional charge in a COEX system is a summary of all the emotions which accompany the memories of the system. Each COEX system has a firm link with particular defence mechanisms. There are both positive and negative systems. Usually people have several COEX systems stored, but the characteristics, extensiveness and intensity vary greatly. Memory constellations in a COEX system are constantly allowed to re-emerge in the therapy sessions until they are fully experienced and may potentially unlock similar systems dealing with other realms of a person's life.

9

The Role of the Therapist
in a Breathing Session

When Rebirthing is used in psychotherapy it is usually combined with conventional therapy methods which can vary between individual therapists. The conscious breathing session functions as an opening to the subconscious. What is released through the breathing can afterwards be analyzed and interpreted in any kind of conventional therapy session. Ingrid Wallin, a psychoanalyst who has successfully used Rebirthing in combination with psychoanalysis for several years, even for patients with serious mental illnesses, says:

> The method gives very good results and is a good way to achieve clarity, to dare to see the worst in oneself. It is a way to link the adult me with the child's frustration, which is very healing. When you dare to take the ghost out of the closet, it will fade away. In the long run the method often gives a deeper outlook on life for the patient, and a greater tolerance, self-esteem and love for one's own person.

Interview with Ingrid Wallin, 1989

Rebirthing is, however, not merely for people with psychological problems. It is mainly practised by 'healthy' people as a cleansing process to clear out past experiences and everyday stress, to relax and to revitalize the body. Despite the diversity of modern human life, most people today need some tool to rid themselves of stress and to regain balance and vitality. In the average conscious breathing session, the technique in itself is sufficient to provoke emotions and memories. But, as stated earlier, the breathing technique is often used in

116

combination with, for instance, 'mind-oriented' techniques, such as visualization, affirmations and dream interpretation, in order to facilitate both the process and the adoption of new behaviour. Since memories are located all over the body, they may also be stimulated by touch, making the combination of Rebirthing with massage or other body-oriented therapies a very versatile tool.

The focus is placed on the natural healing forces of the body, which are merely given the chance to operate freely and to heal what needs to be healed. The healing process cannot be handed over to the therapist at any stage. Even with the most skilled therapist, the outcome and success of the process lies in the person's readiness to maintain open and relaxed breathing.

The rebirther's role during the actual breathing session is mainly to observe and guide the breathing, so that the natural energy cycle is commenced and maintained with an optimal release of energy. A common reaction to too much painful blocking is to choose unconsciously not to breath enough to start the energy cycle. Another reaction is to fall asleep or fade away before the energy cycle is begun. In such cases more precise instructions are needed to overcome the body's defence. The length, connectedness and relaxation of every breath may have to be guided until the threshold of defence is surpassed. This guidance is done 'intuitively', which means that the therapist observes and listens to the breathing pattern in search of the optimal relaxation and openness. Sometimes a gentle massage or other stimulation of particular areas of the body can also be effective.

Although the emphasis is placed upon the technique, rather than the rebirther, the importance of the breathing instructor's skill should not be underestimated. The therapist may intuitively initiate a fine change in the breathing, which leads to an opening and dissolving of energy. A person desiring to become a rebirther must have experienced enough integration of his or her own personal memories to be capable of always being ahead of the rebirthee in this process. A therapist who has not dealt sufficiently with personal subconscious thoughts and emotions may react involuntarily to the process he or she is guiding. The emotions expressed by the rebirthee may trigger similar memories in the therapist, which may start controlling his or her own breathing as a spontaneous reaction of the defence mechanism. Even if the rebirther can still guide the breathing correctly, it will inevitably influence the rebirthee. There is always a subconscious interaction between the two parties in a breathing session: the rebirthee is never allowed to release more than the rebirther personally feels is safe.

If sessions repeatedly encounter these obstacles it may help to open with a discussion of the specific difficulties and how to get in contact with them before the session. It may even be necessary for the session to be conducted sitting up, on the hands and knees, or walking, in order to keep the person conscious of the breathing until the energy cycle starts. Once the natural energy cycle has successfully begun, this feeling of fading usually disappears completely and is replaced with powerful surges of energy throughout the body.

A breathing session is usually followed by a mutual analysis. The aim is not to let the therapist provide the correct answers, but for the rebirthee to find an acceptable interpretation of the experiences. As stated earlier, most of the memories are seen, once they are fully released, as quite harmless childhood memories, from the adult's perspective. An original, vague feeling of discomfort will probably be transformed into the memory of one or several specific events. This makes possible a proper emotional connection, leading to understanding of actions and reactions. Most people will have grown distant enough from their experiences to reach a new understanding and insight. Re-experiencing a memory is therefore a great opportunity to interpret and self-analyze.

A CHANGED ATTITUDE

Even if the average person doing Rebirthing has no special psychological problems, most people need to change their attitude toward themselves, to be able to reach all the blocked material of the subconscious. This can extend from the mere insight that the blocking and integrating of impressions is a constantly ongoing process for all people, to a total change in attitude towards life.

Unfortunately, there are also many general changes in human attitudes that ought to take place outside the Rebirthing session in order to facilitate the personal changes needed. So we must first of all deal with the question of whether a change of attitude by traditional psychology would not facilitate change on a personal level, by generally increasing the area of 'normal' human behaviour. Discoveries, from Rebirthing and other modern deep therapies, clearly indicate the importance of the first phase of our lives, which is not equally emphasized by the traditional theories. As it is today, we are restricted to a narrow spectrum of behavioral patterns, considered 'normal' by established psychology. Their view of the human being is often based on the very mechanistic world view which has dominated the western world for some time now. Often there is not enough tolerance for so-called underlying factors which may influence our behaviour. When someone has an 'irrational' outburst of emotions, it is often diagnosed as a nervous breakdown, with too little consideration of the person's background. The treatment is frequently drugs, which will cause the unwanted behaviour to cease. This may be acceptable in some extreme situations in connection with an acute crisis, provided that it is followed by other treatment that will help the person deal with the underlying causes.

If this is compared with an illustration of treatment for physical injuries, it is easy to realize the problem with this approach to psychological treatment. A person who has broken his arm will gratefully accept the drug that will ease the pain instantly and help him overcome the initial trauma of the accident. But if this person is sent home from the hospital with a mere container of pills to take every time the arm hurts in the future, he will find the treatment utterly unacceptable. An injury of this kind must be dealt with thoroughly to be healed properly, not just disguised by painkillers. X-rays may be needed to identify the extent of the injury, a cast may be needed to support the appendage, or an operation may be necessary. The treatment of an injury or physical illness is often very clear. But when it comes to the psychological aspect of ourselves it is still unclear how to make correct diagnoses and to decide on what treatment to provide. Psychological illnesses, however, must be treated as completely and individually as physical ones. Unfortunately, such treatment is not as simple as putting on a cast. Identifying and altering the underlying factors of psychological problems is not as simple as taking an X-ray. We have still a vast amount to learn about human potential. Therapy may involve several aspects of a person's life: work situation, relations with family and friends, etc. The 'price' of changing an intricate lifestyle may seem too high to pay. Healing may ultimately even include more substantial changes in several areas of the modern social structure, which would have to be dealt with on a political level.

There are, however, several smaller steps that will allow quicker recovery from psychological distress. Perhaps the simplest, but most essential, is to be aware of the fact that nearly every person has at least some suppressed experiences which need to be integrated, and to understand the blocking which this may produce. Even the healthiest person has a subconscious and is thus unable to sort out consciously all underlying thoughts and emotions which form the basis of everyday decisions.

This change in attitude may make it easier to allow people to express pent-up emotions. A person must still be considered sane and rational, and be given an opportunity for self-expression, without causing harm to others, even when his or her behaviour goes outside the 'normal'. Otherwise there will be a feeling of alienation and the lack of a proper forum in the environment to express emotions and suppressed reactions. Such a person needs as much help as would be necessary for a broken arm. If this situation were fully recognized by established psychology, resources might be relocated from traditional hospitals for the sole purpose of this form of healing. Instead of traditional mental hospitals with their time-consuming, expensive treatment for deeply-disturbed people, places might be developed for people to heal themselves by expressing their feelings on a regular basis. (Why not have work-out places for the mind as well as for the body?) This should be done before problems have grown out of proportion and escalated into severe psychological disorders.

A neurotic person is someone who has reached the stage of being totally unaware of the origin of his or her feelings. An agreeable person who never gets angry may actually have more anger than a visibly violent person. The agreeable person may simply be someone whose tight control of blocked material totally seals off any anger. A neurotic person who gets angry with someone will probably not have the courage to show this, without having previously reached some contact with his or her subconscious material. Before that, the anger will be linked with a vague feeling that it has to be controlled. The underlying feeling may be a past fear of displaying anger toward the parents, etc. This person, though provoked into anger by the present situation, does not know that this is a reaction to events in the past, since such emotions are linked with something that has never reached his or her consciousness. Such a person, who has not yet realized or been in contact with blocked feelings, may need a long time to do so. After the first breakthrough of this kind, however, the next stage may be to go straight from the evoking of a feeling to experiencing it consciously. Whilst it can be a long process to reach deeply suppressed feelings, very little is, on the other hand, needed to trigger unexperienced emotions with someone who is about to explode because of them.

Another insight with the power to transform concerns perception. The brain's capacity makes it possible to register an abundance of information during a fraction of a second. In certain situations, for example, we do not only notice the people we meet, the atmosphere and all additional information our senses grant us, but we also 'compute' all this data with our inner reference bank (our conscious and subconscious thoughts and memories). From all this information, we select the parts which hold a certain charge or meaning, increasing or reducing them according to the rest. The whole process occurs so quickly that we do not comprehend that the 'objective' picture created is actually a subjective interpretation. This interpretation frequently leads us to believe that we are facing a repetition of previous events, especially negatively-charged situations. This systematic colouring of our perception happens so often that the brain may be said to have a tendency to recreate specific scenarios. The purpose of this is to equate the present situation with a similar past event blocked in our unconscious, thereby giving the blocked event 'a second chance' to be completely understood and integrated into the inner system.

This understanding in itself can bring about a change in attitude. Instead of perceiving ourselves as helpless victims of a harsh world; as failures, irrational beings with psychological disturbances, we may see ourselves as industrious students eager to learn more about ourselves in every possible situation. Our behaviour can be seen as rational, open to change and focused entirely on the learning process. Our so-called negative behaviour, though remaining unacceptable from a social standpoint, is still rational but totally out of synchronization with the present time. It is rational only as a response to earlier events, hidden and stored in our subconscious.

Forgiveness is an important part of integration, and is in itself a change from negative to positive attitude. To be able to understand the connection between past events and present behaviour will probably make it easier to accept and forgive ourselves. Every time an impression is blocked, it indicates that this impression is unacceptable to the individual. This unacceptability is based on the person's moral and social attitudes which are ingrained since childhood as a set of rules for social behaviour. They are not always based on what is most beneficial for the particular individuals, but are more often concerned with acceptable behaviour as regards our role in society. Some norms are quite harmful, causing unnecessary feelings of guilt and shame. To be able to distinguish clearly the cause and effect in personal behaviour will also help the individual to identify his or her own role in society better and to get rid of unjust feelings of guilt and shame.

A positive attitude toward oneself is manifested in many levels of our being. Chemicals used in medicine can affect the psyche by mixing with the chemical substances of the body. Thoughts can also be described as a form of 'chemical combination' which influences the body chemistry. They trigger a release of various hormone flows throughout the body based on our reactions to our perception of the inner and outer world. These hormones influence our body in a positive or negative way, ranging from what has been termed 'happiness hormones' to 'depressive' effects. Hence, a thought automatically creates a reaction in the body. A negative thought has an inherently limiting effect. A positive thought has the opposite effect.

The difference in the body's reactions to a thought is closely linked with our attitude toward acceptable and unacceptable behaviour. We see the experience of joy as positive and liberating and the experience of grief as negative and restricting. The truth is that we allow the body to act out the feeling of joy fully, while we do our best to conceal and hold back the feeling of grief. It is not as socially accepted to act out negative feelings. To show sorrow, fear, anger and other negative feelings is associated with threats to our personal well-being. It automatically brings us into contact with our own blocked feelings of pain that we do not want to remember. If we are 'successfully' blocking our own emotions we certainly do not want them to be provoked by other people's behaviour.

To accept and express negative feelings is a great step towards change. This does not suggest being totally uncritical towards personal behaviour and acting out all negative thoughts and feelings. A negative feeling of anger can be expressed and released equally well in a positive 'session of wood-chopping' or other physical activity. The important part is to be aware of the feeling, to allow it to be expressed in a harmless way and to 'search' for its origin. The acceptance of all our feelings makes the opening of our blocked, painful experiences more likely. It also gives increased awareness of the behaviour which is necessary to arrive at a full understanding of ourselves. When we perceive a reaction as unacceptable, we automatically close down the possibility of understanding and integrating it. The integration of something is the same as giving up the body's resistance; to allow the thought to mix with the body's energy and flow freely. Then we give the body a chance to heal itself by taking loving care of it and dissolving stored tensions.

Convincing the psyche to accept obvious and positive thoughts may seem unnecessary; one would assume that we automatically change our thoughts as soon as we are aware of them. But the truth is not that simple. Many times the change itself seems threatening. Our basic thoughts are formed so early in our life that we perceive them as inseparable from us. It is as if these thoughts existed before us; that they formed us rather than we formed them. We identify ourselves with our thoughts, behaviour and emotions. When we describe ourselves, we use these thoughts to describe how we look, how we think, how we react, our wishes and dreams. To give up a thought or emotion may be like giving up oneself. So deep is this threat that we would rather stay in the 'safe' negative situation where we at least know who we are, than abandon it because our rational mind knows it is unhealthy. Many people also lack a world view which might provide an alternative, such as a belief in a higher force, to give comfort and security when they give up their previous beliefs.

> We are what our deep, driving desire is.
> As our deep driving desire is, so is our will.
> As our will is, so is our deed.
> As our deed is, so is our destiny.
>
> *Brihadaranyaka IV.4.5*

The Indian school of philosophy teaches the principle of 'neti atma' ('this is not the self'). This refers to those thoughts and attitudes which we see as an inextricable part of our character. By negating the identity of each thought, saying, 'this is not me', the personality is peeled like an onion of layer after layer of thoughts and attitudes. What is left at the end is the true self, seen as the ultimate base of the personality, the ultimate self. By placing the awareness slightly on the outside, in various situations, and becoming something of an observer at the same time as being the actor, a healthy distance and objectivity is initiated. 'I am not my feelings or thoughts'; the 'me' is intact behind the thoughts and feelings. They are merely the consequences and logical answers to what is happening. Through keeping the feeling of 'me' outside of what is happening, one dares to experience more and is less inhibited in reactions. 'I can allow myself to be crazy/afraid/silly/clumsy because it is not me, only my thoughts, emotions and reactions.' (See Part 4.)

THE AFFIRMATION TECHNIQUE

The most important change in attitude which we can achieve, however, is to understand the concept that 'thought is creative'. That is to say, we create our own reality, in the sense that the thoughts which have a great influence in our lives are, in fact, chosen by ourselves. As stated above, our 'objective' picture of the world is, in fact, not always shared by others, but is merely our subjective interpretation. We decide ourselves, to a large extent, if the picture is positive or negative, very much as a result of our attitude to life, rather than the actual situation we are facing. (The car breaking down may be a disaster to the person who hates unexpected incidents, but a positive challenge to the car enthusiast.) This also means that by matching outer impressions with an altered set of thought patterns or attitudes we can actually create a new picture of the world. This understanding is one of the most important insights achieved in modern psychology. The theory that thought is creative is, however, not a new concept. It has been known and used for millennia in the Eastern philosophies (see Part 4).

The practice of conscious breathing enables the release and identification of our thought patterns. An important aspect of this process is the replacement of old negative thought structures with new, positive ones. This may be done with various mental techniques. Two of the most effective and commonly used modes of 'reprogramming' thoughts are the visualization and affirmation techniques. Both work on the principle that a positive result is identified and expressed in such a way that it will influence the brain, either by being visualized through the inner eye, or through writing and verbal repetition of positive statements. Both these techniques are frequently used in areas such as mental training for sports, curing illness, business training (or any other improvement of mental and physical capacities), and/or to promote the positive outcome of a particular challenge.

The most common example of the affirmation technique occurs in advertising. The advertising business has long recognized the effectiveness of this technique, and pours vast sums of money into it each year. These days, hardly any new product is introduced without an advertising campaign to launch it. The average commercial slogan is formulated as a positive statement, exactly as in the affirmation technique. Many slogans simply state a positive fact ('My Toyota is fantastic'). This statement is replicated in as many places and in as many media as possible, as every person on this earth cannot help but notice. The statements are sung, made into anecdotes, filmed, dragged by aeroplanes across the sky. Money and effort is spent to expose the affirmation in as many 'catching' ways as possible. Some large companies will spend enormous amounts of money to have their name linked with, for example, a group of parachute jumpers, a church choir and a football ground full of exercising people. These particular scenes may appear for just a couple of seconds on the TV screen and the use of the product will have no obvious links with these pictures. The main idea is to produce something so different and spectacular that it will make its way into the viewer's consciousness, in competition with all other advertising. In short, everything possible is done to make a chosen statement reach into the minds of people. The reason no efforts are spared in advertising campaigns is that they are clearly proven to be very efficient. Time and again scientists have shown that the brain, in this sense, is similar to a dumb robot which gradually accepts any new idea if it is exposed to it often enough.

The affirmation technique and visualization technique can be said to be private advertising campaigns for personal improvement. Each new concept that we want to introduce into our brain can be launched with an advertising slogan in the form of an affirmation or a mental picture. In short, the technique consists of identifying a positive goal and phrasing it in a short, concise and positive statement or an image. In Rebirthing this is often done through identifying a negative thought pattern and rephrasing it into its opposite, positive meaning. The statement could be 'People love and support me'. This phrase is repeated several times. It can be written, recorded on cassettes, made into a video, a mental picture, painted, placed on the wall in words or pictures. There are any number of creative ways to influence the brain.

By being conscious of any thoughts that come to the mind in association with the statement, subconscious thought patterns can be identified. The positive statement will provoke any negative thoughts a person has towards the goal. A useful exercise is to write down these negative reactions as they appear in the mind. The negative responses can then be used to create new affirmations, to be repeated in the same way. By repeatedly focusing on the positive goal the mind is gradually emptied of its negativity and adjusted to the new concept. This can be compared with focusing on a light, deity or other symbol of the desired goal in meditation.

A Personal Experience

On one occasion I worked on my self-perception through affirmations. It was hard work to write positive statements as, 'My body is radiant with beauty', since I was far too aware that what I wrote was wrong and that I could never change. The more I wrote the more angry I grew. My reactions to the affirmations became increasingly childish, until I felt like an angry, unreasonable child who would like to roll around in dirt, scream and go absolutely mad in order to rid herself of the frustration. The more I regressed emotionally, the faster, and more spontaneous, the writing of the responses became. Page after page was covered with unrelated words and phrases, all expressing childish resentment over not being accepted as I was. It was rage over having to be clean and well-behaved, when I thought it was so much more fun to be out digging in the garden and discovering exciting things. It was anger at always being told I did wrong when I only wanted to do what was most exiting.

One important result of my writing was that I got a new insight into feelings from my childhood. From seeing myself as a timid and quiet child, I experienced an enormous energy and power within me in combination with curiosity and appetite for life.

UNDERLYING FACTORS

Many purely mental exercises are, however, too one-sided, since they focus on acquiring new behaviour without equally stressing the importance of detecting factors underlying the old behaviour. This often works well with a specific problem where a person can be trained to develop one side of their personality by redirecting negative behaviour to another area. There is an old proverb which says 'the sum of your vice is constant'. That is to say, if you get rid of one bad habit you are likely to develop a new one in another area. A person who improves in one area in life may still need some way to express a negative self-image. In other words, our good and bad performance is directly linked with the sum of our self-perception. A person can only be as successful, or destructive, as the sum of their thoughts will allow. Attempted success in one area may mean a compensatory failure in another area. We may actually need less successful sides of ourselves in order to express our negativity. It does not really matter how the success or failure is expressed, as long as it reflects our thoughts. A person who wants an overall improvement will need to identify and integrate the underlying negative constructs in the subconscious to achieve this. The combination of conscious breathing and the affirmation technique is a powerful tool to identify even subconscious thoughts.

Any current thought about the self or one's perception of the world may function as the starting point for an affirmation. Present thought is the sum of all our thoughts and can be traced back to the original conclusion and underlying event. Repeating a positive and seemingly untrue statement, formed from the rephrasing of a negative personal assessment into its opposite, may create an intense reaction within the body and mind. Very crudely it can be compared with advising someone that the best way to learn to fly is by jumping off a high cliff. Any sane person would object violently and demand absolute proof before even considering such a dangerous course of action. But even the simple statement 'people love and support me' may be as dangerous to believe, and cause an equally violent reaction, for a person with many painful experiences of being unloved.

It is important to form the opposite, positive statement of a negative thought, without using a negation. The statement 'I am no longer an unloved person' is too sophisticated for the 'robot brain' to perceive, since the 'processing' of the negations involves another area of the brain. The message perceived will be 'I am an unloved person' which is exactly what is supposed to be changed. The reformed positive statement should be, 'People love and support me'. This should be repeated many times, in various forms, while the responses from the body and mind are noted down.

There are endless examples of negative thoughts which can fill our minds. Here are just a few examples to give a brief illustration:

I have to work hard to make money

I need other people around me to feel safe/happy/satisfied or appreciated

I apologize for my behaviour in order to forego criticism from others

I dismiss compliments from others

I praise others and dismiss myself

I create heroes and see only their good qualities

I look for faults in my appearance, although I know that my models are very unnatural

Such reactions and thoughts do not occur by chance. All behaviour, even the most destructive, is based on absolutely logical deductions formed throughout our lives. This does not mean, however, that they are objectively rational. The logic can only be detected from the viewpoint of their underlying thought patterns. Since a large part of these thoughts are based on subconscious material it can be very difficult to tell what is the cause and effect in everyday thought. It is hard to remember, especially in a familiar environment, that our perception of reality is merely our subjective interpretation of it.

A Personal Experience

During my first trip to India I lost all sense of personal control. Indian society is a loosely-structured chaos, with ancient and modern life interwoven with mystical ideas, yogis that seem to go beyond every known limit of human behaviour, and lots of other unexpected, unbelievable things

mixed into an incredible dreamlike picture. There seemed to be no barriers to life that I recognized. It was slightly overwhelming to say the least.

In those days, my philosophy was to be prepared for the worst in life, to avoid being overwhelmed by it. I had just heard about the creative power of thought for the first time in my life. I was attracted by the idea but did not feel completely safe with it. Instead, my feeling of lost control made me think that if I prepared for the worst I may thereby cause it to happen.

This thought gradually intensified until the week before my departure, when it exploded. I had tried to leave the country earlier than planned, being fully assured it was possible. Still, I was not allowed on the flight due to some error. The next departure was not until a week later. During this week my mind began to truly haunt me. I got more and more obsessed with the idea that my worry created my problems. I just had to find a way to get control of my situation.

I went back to the airline office several times to reconfirm my ticket, and just as an extra precaution I checked that my passport was in order. I found (of course) that it had not been stamped at my arrival in the country and being unable to prove that I actually had arrived and was in the country, I would not be allowed to leave.

This gave added fuel to my mind. I became convinced that I would somehow create new problems and never get out of the country. The departure was in the middle of the night. I might not be able to find a taxi or it might break down on the way out to the airport! To be on the safe side, I reserved a taxi for several hours in advance. The evening before my departure I could not sleep at all.

The taxi arrived on time. So far so good! But after driving a couple of hundred metres down the street the engine gave out a big sigh and died. After half an hour of intensive hammering and banging on the engine, the taxi driver managed to start it and we arrived at the airport far too early anyway. Despite the fact that I was the first one in the check-in line, I had to wait and see all the others walk through the gate. There was something wrong with my ticket. When the counter closed and the plane had taken off I was still there with my bags.

I was told to contact the airline. Their office was closed and no one knew why. I could not find anyone to help me. After a day full of desperate attempts to find anyone to help me, I rushed into another airline and bought a new ticket and went straight out to the airport over five hours early. I could not stand the thought of spending another day in that mad situation. I so wanted to be in touch with my safe Western world again. This time I made it, feeling slightly safer with a 'reliable' European airline to let me on board without problem, and I could return to my organized life, gradually regaining my 'control' in life.

Much more can be said about the affirmation technique. So much that it would require a book in itself to cover the subject properly. There are, however, many excellent books already published, describing the affirmation and visualization techniques more extensively, some of which are included in the literature list at the end of the book.

BREATHING TECHNIQUES IN MODERN THERAPIES

Along with the development of psychology, a deeper understanding of the human brain and behaviour has evolved. Although there seems to be a long way to go yet, before a full understanding of human potential is reached, the last century has seen a piece-by-piece understanding of human potential, which has led to the important insight of how much there is still to learn. Freud made the first important contributions to modern psychology with his identification of the various layers of the human consciousness. Reich followed him, adding the understanding of the body's reactions to the brain. Otto Rank contributed with a wider understanding of the imprint of the birth trauma. Fritz Perls developed a therapy that was based on the importance of acting out emotions. Gradually, all the diverse contributions have led to modern therapies, which involve both body and psyche, through conscious movements, massage, suggestion and breathing. Some have been influenced by yoga and various meditation exercises, while others are based purely on Western psychology. Whatever their origin, they all recognize the importance of openness in breathing in relation to the healing of the psyche. The therapies described here all involve breathing methods similar to Rebirthing.

Along with these therapies, there are a number of other therapies, such as Primal therapy, Aqua Energetics, Radix Neo-Reichian therapy, Feldenkrais body-therapy, Rolfing, Reiki, and Body-Harmony, which put great emphasis on breathing, although breathing is not the main focus of the technique.

ORGON THERAPY

Wilhelm Reich was one of the first psychotherapists to focus on the interaction between the body and the psyche, developing a treatment which involves the whole body. He is generally regarded as the founder of the body-oriented therapy schools. As an apprentice to Sigmund Freud, he used Freud's theories of sexuality as the foundation for his studies on the body's blocking of certain 'negative' feelings. These studies led to the theory of the body's muscular armour and the different emotion zones of the body. He noticed how the body contracts into a defensive position to stop unwanted feelings from reaching consciousness. When such a defence behaviour is maintained for a long period of time it will become chronic. The muscles will be locked into an 'armour', which only therapy can dissolve.

Reich expanded the treatment of patients from a psychoanalytic distance to a more active participation by the therapist. In Freud's method the therapist sat behind the patient, getting him to talk freely about himself, the strategy being to exclude the therapist from the process. Reich, on the other hand, worked in front of the patient, studying the patient's facial expression, body language and gestures. He encouraged his patients to be more articulate in their movements and expressions, in order to get a clearer picture of the unconscious feelings behind them. As a way of breaking the defence mechanism of the patient, he sometimes provoked feelings through his own behaviour or used massage to activate various body zones and get through the muscular armour to reach the underlying feelings.

He realized early the importance of breathing and its influence upon the psyche. During treatment, he instructed his patients to breathe in a deep and relaxed way, all the way down to the genital zone. The first defensive reaction to stop a disturbing feeling, he stated, is to block breathing by locking the ribcage and diaphragm. Reich came to believe that breathing supplies not only oxygen but also a different kind of energy. Still loyal to Freud's theories, he used sexual energy as a starting point for his new theory. To test his theory, he designed various instruments to measure the electric energy raised by the human body. He showed, for example, that human beings produce great quantities of energy during orgasm, and concluded that the orgasmic energy is of great importance for well-being.

It soon became clear to Reich that the same energy is present everywhere in the universe. He therefore constructed further instruments to extract this energy, which he called 'orgon energy', in concentrated form. He built, among other things, a special box where the patient could be exposed to concentrated orgon energy, which he found to be healing and life-giving. His greatest achievement in the use of the box was with cancer patients, where he showed relatively positive results. Reich believed that orgon energy was not only life-preserving but also the beginning of all life. Placing concentrated orgon energy in a totally sterile environment, he was able to produce the microorganisms which provide the basis for all life. This research later received criticism from other researchers in medicine and psychology. Though Reich never made any connections with Eastern theories about life energy, he created his own conceptual system around orgon energy which parallels various Eastern theories.

HOLOTROPIC THERAPY

Holotropic therapy was developed by Stanislav Grof, who is perhaps more widely known for his work with LSD and other drugs. During the late 1950s and early 1960s Grof was involved in pioneering work with drug therapy. After working for a long time with drug-induced experiences, Grof developed a breathing method which resulted in similar experiences. He decided to change his therapy partly because the attitude to drugs became more severe, but also because he found that breathing gave similar experiences without the dramatic side-effects of the drugs.

The deep, strong and rhythmical breathing pattern in Holotropic therapy resembles Rebirthing. During the breathing session, specially selected music is played to stimulate and enhance the emotional reactions. The music is very suggestive, often from various exotic places. Preferably the music should be unknown and wordless to avoid evoking anything other than purely emotional associations. It is played loudly, in order to penetrate and affect both body and mind.

Holotropic therapy is conducted individually or in groups. The person is encouraged to listen inwardly to the signals of the body and to act them out in sounds and movements. As in Rebirthing, the self-healing ability of the individual is encouraged and the role of the therapist is merely to act as a general support or to do focused body work. This means touching or massaging various parts of the body. The focused body therapy is based on the chakra system and the effects of the blocking in the various chakra points (see Part 2).

The focus for Holotropic therapy is not the emotional outbursts, but the emotional experience. The idea is to provoke feelings which have not been fully experienced, to give the body and the psyche a chance to finish the experience. When the emotion is fully experienced it will automatically transform from having a subconscious to a conscious effect on the person. Experiences in Holotropic therapy are very similar to those of Rebirthing. They stretch from present time to the womb, all the way back to what can only be described as experiences from earlier lives. The memories sometimes evoke marks on the body or states of cramp, as Rebirthing does. For the most part, the cramps are experiences around the mouth, and in the arms or hands.

FRANK LAKE REBIRTHING THERAPY

At the same time as Grof was working with LSD therapy in the USA, Frank Lake developed a similar drug therapy in England, which similarly evolved into an alternative method. He used a breathing method based on Reichian breathing patterns. In addition to this he recreated the 'birth situation' with the help of pillows and mattresses. He stimulated the feeling of a narrow womb and birth canal where one could be 'born' again. He also encouraged potential participants to spend time alone, in a small room, in a cave or other environment reminiscent of the womb. The experiences reported from Lake's rebirthing therapy correspond well with the experiences of Rebirthing.

Part 4

THE SPIRITUALITY OF BREATHING

10

Transpersonal Experiences

REBIRTHING AS A SPIRITUAL PATH

Mastery over breath conquers all passion, anger and carnal desires, acquires serenity, prepares the mind for meditation and awakens spiritual energy.

Teachings of Tibetan Mystics

❧

Rebirthing also has an important spiritual aspect. Although the Rebirthing technique has evolved purely from studies of the effect of breathing on the body and psyche, it was soon found to have many similarities with ancient breathing techniques, used to alter consciousness. The ancient techniques have been carefully adjusted over centuries to become precise keys to altered states of mind. During their patient and thorough search for ways to purify body and mind, yogis and other religious searchers discovered and explored the leading role the breathing mechanism plays in the control of the mind. In this way, breathing exercises have become a precise tool for the religious quest. Shamans and medicine men throughout history have used breathing as a way to alter consciousness and to gain knowledge and healing powers. Breathing has revealed itself as the ultimate method of expanding the psyche into other realms.

In the western world, traditional knowledge of altered consciousness has been in decline for many centuries. It has survived only in remote cultures which have maintained their tradition, and among a small number of mystics who have concealed their knowledge in secrecy. Over the centuries, altered consciousness has been perceived as a threat by the church which rejected and/or banned it. Only a couple of hundred years ago witches and magicians were

139

persecuted for their knowledge of the ancient techniques. Still today, practices such as conscious breathing, which may alter consciousness are met with suspicion and fear. There is, however, a tendency in modern science to bridge the gap between science and the spirit. The revelations of quantum physics, above all, have meant a giant step in this direction. In psychology there has been a similar movement towards the recognition of the religious aspects of the psyche. During the 1960s, when psychedelic drugs were studied in psychology laboratories, the spiritual aspect of human experience could no longer be denied. Under the influence of drugs, people reported that they had religious experiences strikingly similar to those described in ancient religious scriptures. Many modern therapies, such as Rebirthing, include the spiritual aspect of the human psyche for the same reason.

The recent recognition of the human psyche, initiated by Sigmund Freud's work, initially made a clear distinction between religion and psychology. Freud, although intellectually interested in religion, merely touched upon the spiritual. In his later revisions of his earlier theories he recognized, however, that certain mental phenomena could be due to a conflict between Eros, the love instinct and creator of higher units, and Thanatos, the death instinct.

Later, Carl Jung reached deeper into human potential, especially in his dream research and the development of 'Jungian analysis'. From his observation of clinical work, he developed the concept of the collective and racial unconscious with its archetypal characters and phenomena. He also introduced the concept of 'synchronicity' – 'the simultaneous occurrence of a certain psychic state with one or more external events which appear as meaningful parallels to the momentary subjective state'. In other words he noticed an abundance of 'inexplicable coincidences' happening to his patients. Some of these coincidences were so striking and outside normal behaviour that they could not be described in other terms than 'psychotic'. His findings led him to a deep involvement in mysticism and a fascination with the ancient Eastern philosophies.

I had the feeling that I had pushed to the brink of the world; what was of burning interest to me was null and void for others, and even a cause for dread.

Dread of what? I could find no explanation for this. After all there was nothing preposterous or world-shaking in the idea that there might be events which overstepped the limited categories of space, time and causality.

Jung, Memories, Dreams, Reflections, 1983

Abraham Maslow also contributed to the non-materialistic theories, with his basic model of human personality. The early stages of his model deal with memories and perinatal traumas. These experiences are followed by the accumulation of new values, motivation, a widened understanding, and the experience of spirituality. Peak performance is the highest level of his chart where a person functions on an optimal level of mental and physical ability and thus experiences feelings of harmony and cosmic union.

TRANSPERSONAL EXPERIENCES

As mentioned earlier, Rebirthing may lead to 'transpersonal experiences', or 'awakening of the kundalini', as it is known in yoga terminology. The expression 'transpersonal experience' is described in Holotropic therapy as 'the expansion of consciousness beyond the boundaries of the ego and the limitations of time and space'. Such experiences lead to the discovery of extraordinary new dimensions of the brain, a new understanding of life, and an increase in personal wisdom. They may also lead to an increase in psychic abilities such as, for example, telepathy, clairvoyance, precognition and out-of-body experiences. (Similar to the reported experiences of awakened kundalini in the Eastern schools.)

These new dimensions are usually reached after numerous Rebirthing session which dissolve layers of stored memories, especially of birth or near-death. Leonard Orr describes this process as 'clearing of the death-urge'. Too many negative thoughts about the self may make a person feel an 'urge' to die, as a way out of his situation. These thoughts are mainly submerged in the subconscious until they are revealed in Rebirthing sessions. They nevertheless have a detrimental effect on a person's behaviour and perception, being the underlying factor for self-destructive behaviour.

There is an 'urgency barrier' in the mind that must be crossed before these deeper layers of consciousness can be reached. This barrier can be breached spontaneously in extreme circumstances, such as life-threatening situations, intense happiness, drug-induced states, or other extreme conditions. This is linked with the often reported experience of 'my whole life unrolling in front of me', when one feels close to death. The urgency barrier can also be passed in a more relaxed and safe way in Rebirthing sessions. When enough tension has been released in the body and in breathing, a sufficient openness is created for these layers to be reached.

Transpersonal experience can sometimes be quite overwhelming and lead to instant changes in the personality, even triggering temporary psychosis. The person may experience a total loss of boundaries, feeling at one with the whole universe, be flooded with love and undergo intensive religious experiences, like meeting God or Jesus. This kind of intense experience can also occur in Rebirthing sessions, and those of other similar techniques. The short-term overwhelming effect of these experiences may be experienced as negative, though the secure and reassuring setting of a Rebirthing session can minimize negative reactions. In the long term, however, such occurrences are generally seen as a positive, powerful part of the personal healing process.

The positive long-term effects of transpersonal experiences are generally unrecognized by traditional psychotherapy. This leads to a lack of understanding and experience in dealing with them properly. People who manifest spontaneous transpersonal experiences, arising from factors in their everyday life, are therefore usually sent to hospital for psychiatric treatment. Even if the experiences occur during traditional psychotherapy they are often regarded as negative and blocked. Traditional treatment is oriented towards blocking this kind of 'psychotic' reaction, with drugs or even electric shock treatment.

Stanislav Grof, among others, is now trying to change such attitudes in traditional psychological diagnoses by advocating the enormous healing potential of this kind of experience. Together with his wife, Christina, Grof has developed a worldwide network of therapists who are trained to deal with 'spiritual emergency'. Their goal is to integrate transpersonal experiences into psychotherapy as a new realm of human potential.

This change in attitude, which these modern therapists are struggling to achieve in the Western world today, has always been recognized in Eastern cultures. They regard transpersonal experience as a major step towards spiritual enlightenment – the ultimate goal. Transpersonal experiences are seen as a short moment of discomfort on the path to inner peace and increased harmony in life. Given these differing perspectives it seems obvious that, to gain a wider understanding of the spiritual aspect of Rebirthing, we need to turn to the East. We shall therefore take a closer look at Eastern spiritual explanations and review the role of breathing in the history of the various ancient techniques.

11

Breathing in Different Cultures:
An Historical Overview

〜

A SEMANTIC APPROACH

The importance which has historically been attached to breath and breathing is reflected in the structure of language itself. In many different languages there is often a clear and close correlation between the words for breath and breathing and the words for soul or spirit: In western Australia the aborigines use the same word *waug* to indicate breath, soul and spirit. In California the Netala-speaking group of American native Indians have the word *piuts* to indicate life, breath and soul. On Java the same word *nawa* is used for breath, life and soul.

Among the aboriginal inhabitants of Greenland two different sources of the human soul are identified: one is the person's shadow; the other is the person's breath. In the Malaysian tradition it is said that the soul of a dying person leaves the body through the nostrils. A Nicaraguan tradition, which was recorded in 1528, gives an explanation of what happens at the moment of death:

> When they die, there comes out of their mouth something that resembles a person and is called 'julio' (from the Aztec word *yuli*, to live). This being goes to the place where the man and woman are. It is like a person but does not die and the body remains here.
>
> *Eliade, From Primitives to Zen, 1967*

Among the Seminoles, the native inhabitants of Florida, when a woman died during childbirth it was the practice to hold up the newborn infant over the mother's face so that it could breathe in part

144

of her soul as it left the body. This would give the newborn part of her strength and knowledge. The Romans had a similar tradition. When a person died the members of the immediate family would lean over the dying person in order to breathe in part of the soul as it left the body. The same tradition can be found in Tyrolean folk songs, which explain that the soul leaves the body through the mouth at the moment of death (Burnett Taylor, 1958).

The Semitic and Indo-European language groups are considered to be the world's oldest. In Hebrew the word *nephesh*, which means breathing is, again, linked to all of the meanings: life, soul and breath. Also the words *ruach* and *neshamah* link together breathing and spirit. In Arabic the words *nefs* and *ruh* mean the same.

In the Slavic languages, the word *duch* has developed from meaning breathing to meaning soul or spirit. In the Romany dialect *duk* means breathing, soul or spirit. The German word *geist* has developed in the same way. In Swedish *ande* can mean soul, spiritual being, or personality, and the word *anda* means the spark of life, breathing, a style of thought and the essential meaning of something. In English the word 'ghost' also comes from 'to breathe'. Similarly, the word 'inspiration' means 'to breathe in' as well as 'to be inspired', and is clearly related to 'spirit', to 'be in spirit' or 'to be in a state of mental arousal'.

CONSCIOUS BREATHING AND ITS AREAS OF APPLICATION

Throughout human history people have engaged in the practice of purposefully changing their pattern of breathing. Traditionally, this was done to achieve three distinct objectives. First, as a means of cleansing the senses (both physically and spiritually), in order to explore their potentialities. Secondly, for medical purposes, as a healing force. And thirdly, for religious purposes, to achieve transcendent experiences and to come into contact with other dimensions of reality. So far we have dealt briefly with the first two of these objectives: the cleansing and healing of the body. Here we shall above all concentrate on the third one, the spiritual purpose.

Many distinct schools, with distinctive techniques of conscious breathing, evolved in all the ancient cultures; mainly in India and China, as we have seen earlier, but also in Persia, Arabia, Egypt, and in ancient Greece and Rome. Many of these cultures also developed some form of conscious breathing as an integral part of their systems of medicine. All of the above-mentioned cultures did, at some point in their histories, have cultural exchange with each other. In the area of breathing technique development, the direction of influence went predominantly from East to West, but there may also have been a certain exchange in the opposite direction. It is most probable that Chinese and Indian theories laid the foundation for the schools of conscious breathing which developed in Greek, Egyptian and Roman cultures. Among all these various ancient cultural traditions of conscious breathing technique, however, it is the Tibetan, the Chinese and the Indian which today exert the most influence. They are still widely practised in their countries of origin and knowledge of them has now also been extensively spread around the world.

Rebirthing has drawn both inspiration and practical guidance from all of these ancient cultures. For practical reasons, however, the following concentrates on the Indian yoga tradition and should be seen as a merely schematic outline of the ancient principles (which are generally similar in each of the various cultures).

From time immemorial in India, there has been a strong interest in the use of conscious breathing and a number of different breathing techniques have been developed throughout the country's history. Conscious breathing has always figured prominently in all the various schools of yoga, as well as in the ayurvedic school of medicine.

The word yoga means union. It has the same origin as the English word 'yoke'. It's aim is union with the cosmic forces and a channelling and controlling of a person's own energies. In other words, the teaching is concerned with how one's own mental and physical powers can be linked together with the universal forces around us. Not much is known about the origins of yoga, or even how old it is. It was probably created and developed, over many generations, by India's aboriginal population. The first evidence of yoga practices were discovered in the pre-Aryan, Harappa culture, which existed in the Indus valley (now part of Pakistan) between 3000 and 1500 BC. This was an advanced civilization which had a written language (which remains undeciphered), and comprehensive trade links with other groups of people. When the Aryans invaded and conquered the Indus Valley in 1500 BC, they absorbed much of the culture of the Harappa, including the practice and theory of yoga.

During the fifth century BC, a wave of movements concerned with spiritual development swept across the Indian subcontinent. It was in the wake of this that the real development of yoga began. During this same period Buddhism and Jainism evolved in India. At the beginning yoga functioned as a practical complement to one of India's six classical philosophical systems, but gradually it became an independent philosophy in its own right. It is not known exactly when the first written description of classical yoga was produced. But it is known that the first personally identified author, Patanjali, was not the founder of yoga but simply described an existing body of theory.

Yoga can be described as a slow and thorough-going cleansing of body and soul. It contains several different methods of achieving this objective. The system of yoga described by Patanjali is nowadays called Raja yoga, i.e. the yoga of thought control. Its starting point, in the effort to reach a higher spiritual level, is the mind. Raja yoga, sometimes called the royal road of yoga, has eight different steps or paths to a higher spiritual consciousness. These different steps involve social and personal rules of living, bodily exercises, breathing exercises and spiritual exercises. All of the steps aim exclusively at teaching the discipline of living in such a way as to achieve union with the absolute.

Hatha yoga is the yoga of body control. Hatha yoga's starting point is the body. The word Hatha is composed of 'ha', meaning the sun, the positive energy or aspect, masculine form, and for inhalation of breath, and 'tha' which means the moon, the negative energy or aspect, feminine form and the exhalation of breath. 'Ha' also represents the esoteric aspect and 'tha' the body. The assumption behind Hatha yoga is that if the mind can influence the body, then the body can also influence the mind: it is seldom the case that a person suffers from physical tension without having mental tension or stress, though it is nearly always the case that the mental tension appears first and causes the physical tension.

Yoga contains certain concepts which are completely absent from Western categories of thought. In the East the world has, for thousands of years, been observed from a subjective perspective, using the inner experiences obtained from yoga and meditation. This is something which the Western world has only recently begun to apply, mainly thanks to developments in modern physics. Before these developments, there was simply no reason to try and account for phenomena which did not fit in with the materialistic world view, which makes a sharp distinction between body and soul. 'Prana' (Sanskrit for absolute energy) is perhaps the most important concept in yoga.

Prana is the ground principle of energy; the cosmic life force which pervades every atom in the universe. Everything that happens in the universe, everything we do and think, can (potentially) happen in harmony with the cosmic life force, which means that it happens in the most perfect way. In such a case no energy is consumed; nothing is broken down or worn out. There is a total openness and balance in the stream of energy on all levels, from the microcosmos to the macrocosmos. Prana stimulates growth in all living organisms at the level of the smallest cells. It is prana that signifies the difference between living things and lifeless things. Everything living requires prana in order to exist.

Prana exists everywhere and can be absorbed by the body via the food we eat, via our skin, but above all through breathing. But prana is not the same as oxygen. It is rather prana that gives oxygen its life-giving quality. If one breathes in a concentrated way with a relaxed body and openness of the mind one can come into contact with one's 'inner breathing'. This is a type of 'mental breathing' which enables the body to absorb prana more effectively from the environment. The nearest parallel, in modern Western thought, to the concept of prana is the electromagnetic radiation which is thought to form the basic energy in the smallest particle and which exists as background radiation throughout the universe.

Pranayama is the name of the breathing exercises which are a central part of yoga. The word pranayama is a combination of prana (energy) and yama (exercise). Hatha yoga contains a large number of different bodily exercises and cleansing processes, all of which are intended to clean and discipline the body for a higher spiritual state. In all of these exercises, enormous importance is placed on breathing in the correct way.

> Eminent authorities have stated that one generation of correct breathers would regenerate the race, and disease would be so rare as to be looked upon as a curiosity. Whether looked at from the standpoint of the Oriental or Occidental, the connection between correct breathing and health is readily seen and explained.
>
> *Yogi Ramacharaka, The Hindu-Yogi Science of Breath*

There are, in addition, a large number of special breathing exercises designed, for example, to enable the body to absorb extra prana, or to release the dormant kundalini energy. An individual who awakens the kundalini in his body gains access to other dimensions of reality. The effects of pranayama can be found described in even the earliest writings on yoga:

> By Pranayama is attained the power of levitation (Khechari Sakti),
> By Pranayama diseases are cured,
> By Pranayama the Sakti (spiritual energy) is awakened,
> By Pranayama is obtained the calmness of mind and exaltation of mental powers (clairvoyance, etc);
> By this, mind becomes full of bliss;
> Verily the practitioner of Pranayama is happy.
>
> *The Gheranda Samhita verse 57*

Pranayama is an extremely well-known concept in India. In the *Bhagavad Ghita*, which is the most prominent and most widely-read of the classical Indian scriptures, one can read about the importance of pranayama:

149

> Some offer the inward breath in the outward,
> Likewise the outward in the inward,
> Checking the flow of both,
> On breath control intent.
>
> *Bhagavad Ghita 4:29*

Unlike Rebirthing, breathing in pranayama is most often slow, and without connection between inhale and exhale. In pranayama one strives to make the pattern of breathing slow. At some points, one is even required to stop breathing altogether. Breathing should be rhythmic. Its phases should be divided up in the following way: inhalation, the holding in of the breath, and exhalation. These three stages should each take about the same length of time. In certain pranayama exercises, however, one breathes faster than normal. This drives carbon dioxide out of the blood while, at the same time, powerfully enriching its oxygen content: a combination which has proved to have a calming effect on the breathing centres in the brain and entire sympathetic nervous system.

The yoga tradition contains a holistic view of the human body and psyche. Traditionally, the exercises for inner development take place within the context of a special form of teaching, communicated by a guru. Guru means a teacher or a master within the yoga tradition. Distinctions are made between guru (teacher), sad guru (the great guru), parama guru, who is higher than a sad guru, and patmatsdi guru, the highest guru. Because yoga is a teaching which leads to a higher state of spiritual development, it is essential that those teaching yoga have themselves reached the spiritual level which they wish to transmit to others. (This criterion can also be applied to rebirthers.) The guru functions as a catalyst for the student and as a mediating link to higher states of consciousness.

The student strives to develop physical abilities which in the West are regarded as supernatural. It is therefore not always necessary that the guru and his student meet each other in physical form. Telepathic guidance can take place in different forms. An essential element in the relationship between the guru and the student is that it is the student himself who seeks out his guru and then remains responsible for maintaining a living contact with the guru.

Yoga has now been firmly established all over the world. In the West Hatha yoga is the most common form practised. To a certain extent it has, however, become separated in the West from the great spiritual framework within which it was developed. It tends to be seen merely as a system of exercises to achieve personal maturity, physical or psychological relaxation, or as a method for resolving certain physical problems.

THE MANY FACES OF KUNDALINI

Since the 'awakening of kundalini' plays an important part in the expansion of consciousness beyond its normal boundaries, we shall have to look more deeply into its role in ancient spiritual exercises.

Although the concept of kundalini (and its equivalents in other cultures) is central to the process of attaining a higher awareness, the awakening of kundalini is not the goal in itself. But it is an essential step towards an expanded consciousness or enlightenment. The awakening of kundalini initiates the cleansing/expansion process which enables the psyche to expand beyond its present level.

Its significance is evident in the numerous detailed descriptions of the awakening of kundalini in the Indian and Chinese schools, although these are not the only ones. Similar accounts occur frequently among Christian mystics, Sufis and native people throughout the world. Although the terminology may differ, many tales from Egyptian and Greek mythology illustrate the awakening of kundalini. Isis the Egyptian earth mother (whose symbol is the curled up snake) and Osiris have a close link to kundalini powers and can be seen as the Egyptian equivalents to Shiva and Shakti.

Older literature often provides interesting and detailed stories about a deeply religious person's path to God. The reports are often about young women. They describe fights with the devil or intensive experiences of Christ or God. These experiences are very similar to the awakening of kundalini. The event often starts with intensive prayers, periods of fasting or ascetic practices. The symptoms include inexplicable illnesses with high fever, shivering, cramps, spasms, hallucinations, temporary insanity. The illness usually disappears as quickly and inexplicably as it appeared.

A book published in the 1300s tells the story of a young woman's religious quest – the blessed maiden Kristina of Stommeln. She had many religious experiences with strong physical and psychological reactions. One passage has an extended account of such an experience, which could also serve as an account of spontaneous Rebirthing:

> When she had been sitting like this, slightly leaned forward on the bench, with her face and hands covered by a veil, for about three or four hours, she suddenly sighed, so that the body was put into a light movement. She slowly began to breathe, though slower and lighter than people usually breathe. Her breathing was so slow and unusual that only with the utmost attention could it be noticed. She took, as I said, a breath in a much quieter and lighter way than normal, but the time that elapsed between inhalation and exhalation was, in spite of this (which seems contradictory), much longer that usual. When she had been sitting like this for about the time required for two masses, she gradually began to breathe deeper in a conventional way. Then she started talking, but still so softly that it could hardly be discerned by the most perceptive listener and not in coherent sentences, but with disconnected phrases, pet names and love words such as 'you highly beloved', 'the most precious', 'my most beloved', 'darling' and 'bridegroom', seeming to rejoice with mysterious shivering, so that her whole body shivered and remained in this shivering rejoice longer than a Miserere, all this in one and the same breath, whereby she again became immobile, though not for as long. This state of laughter, shivering, bliss and joy – I don't know how to describe it, since I have never seen anything like it before – lasted, I think, as long a time as two masses. Her onlookers were brought to tears through the incredible holiness and burning love, which she hereby gave multiplied expression to.
>
> de Dacia, *Om den Saliga Jungrun Kristina av Stommeln*, 1965

Rituals of native people are similarly aimed at provoking the kundalini forces. The men of the !Kung tribe from the Kalahari desert dance for hours to 'warm up n/um' in order to reach the state of '!kia'. 'N/um' greatly resembles kundalini. '!Kia' is the same as a transcendental state and is used to dissolve tension, gain mental clarity and power, and for healing. 'Rapid shallow breathing is what gets out n/um . . . then n/um gets into every part of the body from the tips of the toes to the roots of the hair'. An eye witness gives another vivid picture of the ritual dance:

> At first the rhythm is restrained, but one can sense the enormous tension, as if a flood of energy is being held back tightly controlled . . . One feels the power of millennia past, reaching out to tug gently at the soul and strange responses start from within . . . To them, the trance world is real, and survival in the living world is dependent upon successful communication with the non-living world.
>
> *Main, Kalahari, 1987*

The !Kung tribe has been carefully studied over the years, because they have been able to maintain their ancient lifestyle more or less intact over the ages. They also inhabit the region of the world where the oldest traces of human history have been found. They have, among others, been subject to many medical studies. A special reason for this is that they have been said to have several supernatural abilities. It is therefore possible to provide a medical explanation as to why the trance occurs through the dancing:

> Hours of energetic dancing attune every muscle to the rhythm, and there is an exact and monotonous balance between demand and supply of oxygen. In order to induce a state of trance, the dancer shortens his breathing, without reducing the level of his physical exertions. An oxygen deficiency is created which leads to drowsiness and profuse sweating. The heart pumps more strongly in order to circulate the blood through the lungs more rapidly and, at the same time, blood pressure in the brain is increased.
>
> *Bjerre, Kalahari, 1960*

The only decisive criterion for becoming a 'n/um' master is the process in itself, but it helps to have a rich imagination and sensibility. Everyone who experiences 'n/um' and can reach the '!kia' state automatically becomes a 'n/um' master. Although the dancing starts spontaneously, it is only done by the men. The women sit around in a circle, clapping and encouraging the dancers. The state is more easily accessible to some, especially the elders who can enter the trance almost at will.

The zazen or the zen meditation school has the concept of 'makyo' ('ma' meaning the devil, 'kyo' meaning the objective world). This is described as diabolical phenomena occurring at some point, when meditation is used for spiritual development. Makyo is a mixture of real and unreal phenomena, similar to dreams. It includes visions, hallucinations, phantasies, dreams, pictures, sound, smell, or homeostatic changes (body temperature and sweating, etc) – all of which are said to be caused by the breathing not being in harmony with the mind. When the mind has been stilled only partly, deeper-lying thoughts from the unconscious reach the surface and are expressed in pictures and visions.

In Tibet, the dormant kundalini force is known as 'thig-le' (the essence), or blocked wisdom. The liberation of the 'thig-le' is the main route to the expansion of consciousness. The Tibetan school distinguishes between the physical and subtle (psychic) body, the latter having numerous subtle channels which form a crucial link between psychic and physical bodies. The main objective of these channels is to transport psychic forces – air and essence, the concentrations of energy. A complex interaction occurs between the various body regions. The body depends on the psychic channels. The channels in turn depend on the psychic forces, which subsequently depend upon the mind. Emotions support the psychic forces, the psychic forces support the channels and the channels support the body. But the psychic forces control everything, like a wild untamed force. The average person has his wisdom tangled in energy concentrations which block the subtle channels, with a negative and limiting effect. The blocked 'thig-le' can be released and controlled through breathing and other yoga exercises. When 'thig-le' is released it is transformed into wisdom for the person and is described as a direct pathway to the realization of Buddhahood (enlightenment).

THE CONCEPT OF THOUGHT AS A CREATIVE FORCE

Transpersonal experience is not the only Rebirthing concept which can be explained by the spiritual philosophies of the East. This is also true of the creativity of thought, which plays a central role in Rebirthing. In the East, the concept of the creativity of the mind can be traced back in literary sources, at least as far back as Buddha, who stated:

> We are what we think.
> All that we are is started in our thoughts.
> With our thoughts we will make the world.
>
> *Dhammapada*

The creative power of the mind has always had a central role in the Eastern philosophies, as well as in other ancient cultures throughout the world. Being able to fully understand and subjectively experience how our thoughts influence our lives has always been an essential step to enlightenment. Given this, various techniques for training and controlling the thoughts have been used in the East for thousands of years.

Because the spoken word is a direct reflection of what we think, consciousness of what we say is an important method of thought control. Although it was developed very early on, human beings have not always had a spoken language. Primitive humans had very simple sounds, similar to monkeys and other sound-producing animals. The first 'words' were probably imitations of the original sounds which they referred to. The development of language lasted for several thousand years. It is assumed that the development was comparable to the child's acquisition of language. Imitation was followed by single words, which were formed into simple sentences and so on.

The creation of language was a great milestone in human

development. It led to the discovery of a new world, the inner world where the word was an expression of the soul. Every word was the resounding equivalent of an inner experience. By uttering a specific word it was possible to bring the personal will outside the mind to make it influence the external world. The word could also enable the entrance to a world beyond the apparent by making it possible to share the inner world of someone else. People could discuss their thoughts and perceptions of the world with others. A whole group of people could combine their mental capacity to find solutions and make discoveries. This is reflected in a quantum leap in human evolution. Fossils of this assumed time period indicate an explosive growth in the style and complexity of human culture. It is furthermore believed that all existing languages have been developed from one single original language.

> Since the advent of the computer, we can now figure out with the aid of the laws of probability whether an event can possibly be accidental. If we do so here, we will find that 'chance' would not have had enough time, because the phenomenon of human language is simply not old enough. For the god of chance to have created not only sporadic, random word similarities across our planet but a series of complex order, the dinosaurs would have had to have a language – a human language – long before Homo sapiens came into existence, millions of years before the appearance of Homo erectus.
>
> *Berendt, Nada Brahma The World is Sound, 1987*

All the modern Western languages come from six original groups (Latin, Slavic, Greek, Sanskrit, Germanic, Keltic) which have developed over the last 7,000 years. The belief in the power of the word was still strong when the Latin and Germanic languages were developed. This is constantly reflected in the original meanings of words. Here are just a few examples:

> The Latin word *cantare* (to sing) originally meant 'to create through magic'. The root is still seen in words like *carmen* (poem), the original meaning of which was a magical formula.

The English word 'name' originally signified the declaration of an oracle, similar to the Germanic word *edda* which means 'myth'. This is, in turn, related to the Germanic *nef-na* (to give name) which may also have the deeper meaning of 'to solemnly proclaim'.

The word 'speak' can be linked with the Latin *preces* (prayer), in turn linked with the Sanskrit *brihaspati*, related to 'Brahma', (the highest god to whom people pray). Brahman is also linked with the Nordic god Brage.

Very early on, cultures implemented techniques to influence and control thoughts. One of the most important ways to control the mind is to constantly repeat positive words and phrases – mantras (Indian word for affirmations). The word mantra consists of 'man' (to think) and 'tra' (tool). Mantra is a 'tool to think'. The spoken word is a reflection of a thought, but its influence works both ways. When the mantra is repeated it creates a mental picture of the meaning of the word. A mantra usually consists of a name or quality of higher beings, gods or powers, since the mythological gods symbolize human qualities. If the mantra is repeated with total concentration and vivid realization, it evokes their corresponding qualities in the body and mind.

Mantras can be repeated in silence or aloud, during meditation, to still the inner thought process completely. In order to still the thought process the thoughts are first allowed to flow freely. The repetition of a mantra will function as an aid to focus the mind and simultaneously create an inner picture of something positive. Then a state of mind without worries, desires, needs or any kind of disturbing thoughts can be attained. Once the thought process is stilled, we are able to exist only in the here and now. Being totally focused on present time is the best way to reach beyond the normal state of mind to a higher consciousness. Without any distracting thoughts that will link us with a certain image of ourselves, we can more easily realize our union with God. This experience will help us see that once we let go of our thoughts we can reach a state of harmony and peace. This will in turn help to detach the mind from everyday life. It will make it easier for us to see our role as creator of our thoughts.

> He who can pronounce it (Aum) with the right tone, is able to work wonders, and he who knows how to utter it silently, attains supreme emancipation.
>
> David-Neel, Alexandra, Magic and Mystery in Tibet, 1984

The most powerful of all mantras – the supreme mantra – is 'Om' (Sanskrit) or 'Aum' (Tibetan). This is the symbol for the 'Inexpressible Absolute'. It is described as the original sound, the vibrations of which created the world.

Even the Christian religion regards thought, or the word, as the origin of our world.

> In the beginning was the Word, and the Word was with God, and the Word was God.
>
> The same was in the beginning with God.
>
> All things were made by him; and without him was not any thing made that was made.
>
> John 1:1-3

To pray is the same as to repeat an affirmation or mantra. The Christian rosary used for the repetition of God's name probably has the same origin as the mala (Indian rosary with 108 beads used as an aid in the repetition of a mantra). If a prayer is delivered with full attention and concentration, 'God will listen and fulfil it'.

The power of the spoken word has also been described in terms of physics. On the micro level, human beings consist of atoms that vibrate with a certain frequency, emitting a particular sound. The sound and vibrations created by a spoken word influence the vibration frequency of the body's atoms, and thus influence the person as a whole. (Various moods also give rise to various different frequencies.)

> Each atom perpetually sings its song, and the sound creates each moment dense or subtle forms. Just as there exist creative sounds,

there exist destructive sounds. He who is able to produce both can, at will, create or destroy.

David-Neel, Alexandra, Tibetan Journey, 1960

Modern technology has even verified this theory of the sound. The 'harmony of the spheres' has been confirmed by studies of space which have shown that a 'cosmic symphony' is constantly playing in the universe. Each planet, star, sun and moon, everything in space gives out a special sound and rhythm depending on how it vibrates and moves. The resonance of the planets has even been registered and recorded by several observatories.

MAGIC WRITING

Another great milestone in human history, which is linked with the creative mind concept in Rebirthing, is the development of written language. This meant that a person's thoughts could be transferred to scriptures that survived even after the author's death. The idea could be passed on to others and multiplied without any involvement from the person who first expressed them. Written language originally was only taught and used by magicians, shamans and medicine men to express their magical words and symbols. By writing them they charged the letters with their special powers. Egyptian hieroglyphs and Nordic runes are two examples of languages used as tools in magical rites to provoke the human powers through altered states of consciousness. These unique powers were perceived even after writing spread to wider groups. In the Scandinavian countries the tradition of using runes or symbols survived in remote places up until the last century. A stick or plate with runes or similar symbols was often hung over the front door of a house to bring luck to it (like the horseshoe). It could also be used as a tool to bring good fortune to any everyday project, like milking the cows.

Every godly word came to be through the heart's thought and the tongue's bidding. When the eye sees, the ear hears and the nose breathes, they report to the heart. It is the heart that brings out every flood of words and the tongue that repeats every thought of the heart. Thus all the gods are being imaged from Ahrm and further.

Text from 8th Century BC Egyptian stone plate

The modern affirmation techniques (or any other learning process) also give a sort of magic importance to written words. They all recommend that positive statements are written down as well as spoken. This locks them firmly in the memory and thereby increases their influence. In order to transform something into written words we must absorb it into the brain, analyze and interpret it, to be able to reproduce it. As long as we are not dealing with a foreign language which we do not understand, we become involved in the whole process of understanding and rephrasing a sentence in order to copy it, instead of just trying to copy the shapes of the letters. The more senses which are involved, the greater the impact on the brain. It is easier to remember something that has been processed in both the linguistic region of the brain and the region which physically coordinates the writing. This process leaves a certain imprint in the brain, which eventually affects our thought processes.

KARMA

One of the most frequent and profound questions arising from the practice of Rebirthing concerns personal identity. 'Why did I develop this personality when the rest of my family is so different?' Modern psychology provides little explanation, apart from the influence of heredity, family role play, etc, as to why people from the same background develop totally different personalities. The Eastern philosophies on the other hand have a wider world view and are therefore able to offer more extensive explanations. One concept in particular, not widely recognized in the West, but of vital importance in the ancient cultures, can help to address such questions. This is the concept of Karma, which explains the factors underlying cause and effect in human life.

In the Eastern philosophies the concept of the creative power of the human mind is closely linked with the theory of karma. The concept of karma makes it possible to place human behaviour in its correct context. It provides a proper understanding of how the human mind can influence reality. Although the word 'karma' is associated with Eastern religions, karmic theories are not exclusive to these philosophies. The theory of karma can be found in the Christian religion as well. Though its role has decreased over the years, descriptions of karma are discernible in the Bible. Jesus frequently depicts karma. For example:

As you sow, so shall you reap.
With whatever measure you mete out to others,
with the same measure it shall be meted out to you.

Matthew 7:2

Karma can be said to show the guidelines for how our life may turn out. The law of karma determines the relationship between cause and effect in the universe. This is one of the cornerstones of the ancient philosophies, and forms the basis for guiding human behaviour along the religious path. It is described in numerous different contexts.

Like the Buddha, the sages of the Upanishads did not find the world capricious. Nothing in it happens by chance - not because events are predestined, but because everything is connected by cause and effect. Thoughts are included in this view, for they both cause things to happen and are aroused by things that happen. What we think has consequences for the world around us, for it conditions how we act.

Eknath Easwaran, Introduction to Dhammapada, 1986

All creation, every phenomenon in the universe, has an underlying blueprint in the form of Dharma (from the Sanskrit word *dhri* - to bear or hold, indicating the quality that 'holds together').

Probably no word (dharma) is richer in connotations. In the sphere of human activity, dharma is behaviour that is in harmony with this unity. Sometimes it is justice, righteousness, or fairness; sometimes simply duty, the obligations of religion or society. It also means being true to what is essential in the human being: nobility, honour, forgiveness, truthfulness, loyalty, compassion.

Eknath Easwaran, Introduction to Dhammapada, 1986

Sanatana Dharma (the eternal dharma or the original righteousness) is also the Indian name for religion. The goal of religion is to live in harmony with the eternal dharma. Anything deviating from this will disturb the natural balance, thereby creating karma.

The Taoist explanation of the law of karma involves the concepts of yin and yang. They are the opposing forces, expansion - contraction, which cooperate to give rise to all phenomena in the universe. In Taoism there are three main principles ruling everything in the universe.

The first principle says that the force of yin attracts the force of yang to reach a state of balance. This applies to all situations where the forces attract each other, from magnetic energy fields to the attraction between people which we call love.

The second principle says that forces of the same kind repel each other to give place for opposite forces to meet.

The third principle says that when either yin or yang reaches a climax it transforms into its opposite force. This principle is reflected in the human life cycle, and in the seasons of the year. It also explains how thought or energy may be transformed into matter.

If these principles are followed everything is done in harmony with the universe. This means that no karma is created. It is a difficult situation to reach since the brain is constantly producing new thoughts that disrupt the natural order, and thus create karma. Negative karma leads to a destructive process that strives to destroy everything which is not in harmony with the original 'blueprints' of the universe, to make room for a new situation where it can be reformed in a more perfect way. A common goal for the ancient (or, as Aldous Huxley called them, 'perennial') philosophies is to reach a state of liberation that gives freedom and total harmony with the universe. A return to the Garden of Eden, to use a Christian metaphor. Buddha said:

> Everything is forgone by the mind,
> led by the mind,
> created by the mind
>
> *Dhammapada*

Every time we form a thought it puts energy into motion. Every thought forms the energy in a unique way. This is the same energy that causes all phenomena to occur in the universe. If the motion in the energy is strong enough and clearly formed, it will cause phenomena that can be perceived with our senses. If the motion is weak it will only influence the form and character of other phenomena that the stronger forces have created.

> That energy, they (the Tibetan mystics) believe, is produced every time that a physical or mental action takes place. - Action of the mind, of the speech and of the body, according to the Buddhist classification. - The production of psychic phenomena depends upon the strength of that energy and the direction in which it is pointed.
>
> *David-Neel, Magic and Mystery in Tibet, 1984*

New light has been shed upon this ancient explanation in recent years, through modern technology. Quantum physicists have shown that all phenomena in the universe can be reduced to only a few hundred various types of particle, described as energy, expressed in complex patterns of probability waves. This energy can be expressed simultaneously as a particle or as a wave. Matter does not exist with any certainty, but rather 'shows tendencies to exist'. In the same way events do not occur but they merely 'show tendencies to occur'. On this level every phenomena in universe is identical.

This leads to the origin of the concept of creative thought, which is linked with the creation of the universe itself. The ancient theories of how the universe was formed correspond surprisingly well with the modern 'Big Bang' theory. The Taoist explanation divides the universe into seven levels - seven heavens (a well-known expression even in the Western world) which are comparable to modern physics' classification of the particles of microcosms to the largest entities of macrocosms. The first heaven is the physical world. The following levels encounter smaller and smaller entities. The seventh heaven is the timeless eternity, God, Wholeness, the Absolute and Omnipresent.

Modern theories state that before the Big Bang - the beginning of the universe - there was no time or space, form or dimension. In the first phase of the big explosion, the heat was so intense that only endless movements in all directions could exist. As the universe cooled, the movement started to take on the form of various patterns. Gradually small particles evolved. As it cooled still further the particles formed bundles held together by electromagnetic energy fields.

The first movements that were formed after the Big Bang are the same as the yin and yang movements, which form the basis for everything in the universe. They cannot be separated into entities and have not changed since the time they first occurred. They move in a timelessness that links everything together from the beginning of universe to its possible end.

This brings us back to the law of karma - the law of cause and effect. On the micro level thought is a movement in energy, like all other movements of energy that cause phenomena to occur in the universe. What separates the invisible thought from solid matter is that thought energy can be found only on the micro level. Through thinking, energy is put into motion, which influences the movement on the micro level. If the influence is strong enough, it will transform even the larger parts. If the influence is small, it will only change the character of the larger parts.

MAYA

Many of the transpersonal experiences in Rebirthing also involve the spontaneous revelation of an inner, previously unknown 'source of wisdom', resembling Jung's collective unconscious. Jung's theory of a collective unconscious was based largely on his studies of dreams. It describes the source of endless wisdom, accessible to all human beings at certain times, especially during dreams or deep relaxation.

In the Eastern philosophies, it is an expanded collective unconscious and the inner experience of union with everything in the universe which is regarded as the true reality. It is our everyday world, our 'reality', which is the illusion, called 'maya' in Sanskrit. Maya is the 'tip of the iceberg' of our thoughts. The world we perceive as the real world is created by our other levels of consciousness. It is formed by individual human thoughts in combination with the collectivity of all human thought. This does not, however, make maya an hallucination. When the energy of these thoughts is sufficiently strong, it will become material. Once transferred into matter, objective reality is formed following the inherent laws of physics. Time, in this context, is a subjective image created by our minds. As Lama Govinda (1960) states: 'We do not live in time but time lives in us'.

> Most people think that time is moving. In reality it stands still where it is. The thought that time is moving is false since the human being is limited to experiencing that time moves and does not understand that it stands still.
>
> *Dogen, Japanese master of Zen*

Several similar theories have been developed by modern physics. Einstein's now famous theory of relativity states that there is no distinction between time and space, only an illusory one. Everything is interwoven in a four-dimensional continuum referred to as 'space–time'.

> For a convinced physicist as myself, the separation between the past, present and future is just a stubborn illusion.
>
> *Albert Einstein*

Through the theory of relativity, Einstein was also able to demonstrate that pure energy can generate material particles and vice versa. Geoffrey Chew (1968) introduced another famous approach, 'the bootstrap philosophy', for a type of subatomic particle. He states that

165

the universe is an infinite web of mutually-interrelated events, all parts of which reflect the properties of the other part. From this perspective all theories of natural phenomena may be seen as creations of the human mind.

The idea that the observed phenomena and the observer are part of the same entity is firmly established in modern physics, as well as in the ancient scriptures. Based on the physical laws of nature, quantum physicists conclude that through observing the universe we may also create it.

> What is within us is also outside us
> What is outside us is also within us
> *Upanishads*

In modern biology there is a similar approach in many new theories. Earlier, the main theory of life was mechanical, seeing living organisms as physiochemical machines. This view dominated biology for over one hundred years. Many of today's critics claim that there are good reasons to question whether many phenomena in life, including human behaviour, can ever be explained totally mechanistically. There is an on-going search for a theory that can explain qualities and factors which are, at the present time, unknown to physical science.

Sheldrake (1985) has put forward the hypothesis that there is a kind of power field (morphogenetic field) which gives everything its characteristic form, in biology as well as in chemistry and physics. This energy field may cause physical changes despite the fact that it is impossible to identify in itself. It is also presumed to influence and control the changes of appearance and behaviour of species (formative causation). Experiments have shown that rats which are taught a new skill tend to learn it easier once one of them has mastered it. It also becomes increasingly easier for following generations to learn this particular behaviour pattern (morphic resonance). The more rats who learned the new behaviour, the easier it became for the remaining rats. This was also the case when the experiment was carried out simultaneously in different places around the world. If rats in a particular country had mastered the new skill, it became easier for rats elsewhere, although there was no physical contact between the different groups.

The concept of time plays an important role in this theory. Sheldrake assumes that each moment is a projection of the whole, which contains a kind of memory of all earlier moments. The proceeding moment will be a new, slightly upgraded projection of the whole, since it now contains one more memory of an earlier moment. This means that everything that occurs in one place will have an effect in other places as well. Everything that happens in a specific moment will return to influence the totality before it is projected into the next moment.

As a further explanation of thought transmission, Berendt (1987) describes how photons (one of the smaller particles in microcosms) may carry messages.

> The fact that electrons, as microcosmic particles, are smaller in size than we can imagine does not speak against their unimaginably large capacity for information storage . . . the number of photons in an electron is almost unlimited since the mass of the electron is incredibly dense . . . A simple computation by Charon (mathematician) shows that even in this moment, towards the end of the twentieth century, each one of us, with each breath we take, exhales or inhales a few dozen of the same electrons that Julius Caesar expelled with his last sigh at the moment of his assassination in 44 BC. Our assumption that an electron stores everything that has taken place since the beginning of the universe does not just apply to some random electrons way out in the depth of cosmic space. A few of the 'oldest' electrons are in each one of us. And each one of us, therefore – the repetition is intentional – has electrons that have been part of Jesus or the Buddha or other great saints and seers in history, electrons that are charged with their photon information, their photon cognition, their photon love. In each one of us, on the other hand, are also electrons that have been in (and are thus programmed by) people like Hitler and Stalin, Himmler and Eichmann and other arch-criminals of mankind.

Indeed, even from this vantage point we seem to be headed toward the realization of the seers and wise men of Asia and Egypt that everything is in us – the same realization that is suggested by modern theoretical physics and holography.

Berendt, Nada Brahma The World is Sound, 1987

There have been several attempts made to objectively study collective consciousness theories. For example, studies of TM (transcendental meditation) have tried to measure the transmission of thoughts between people. The results show that relatives, and people in close contact with each other, react to one anothers' thoughts with changes of the alpha waves in their brains. In one study, a group of people practising TM meditation caused a control group at a distance of 1500km to react with changes in their brain activity. The brain activity of the control group was gradually synchronized with the meditating group, in such a way that both groups activated the same parts of the brain.

REINCARNATION

Many of the transpersonal experiences derived from conscious breathing concern reincarnation and karma. It is one of the five large areas of experience which have been identified over Rebirthing's twenty-year history. Even if a person is not familiar with these concepts, he or she may still describe the experience as being pictures from previous lifetimes. The pictures may occur in an historical environment, in which the rebirthee takes part himself. Sometimes they contain more detail than the person's conscious knowledge of history could conceivably create. Often the scenes illustrate some event that can be related to the person's present life situation. The picture often functions as an aid to clarify or connect present behaviour with some meaningful background. Seen in this wider context the question of a person's special life situation and personality may thereby be brought into a totally new perspective. Since these types of experience lack a satisfactory explanation in Western psychology, they are sometimes simply dismissed as 'abnormal' phantasies. However, experiences of this kind occur frequently in Rebirthing. If they are approached via the perspectives of karma and reincarnation, they can create a useful distance from any personal trauma involved. In Rebirthing (as in the East) they are therefore regarded as useful tools for personal development. Consequently, as a final stop on our Eastern excursion, we shall explore this subject a little further.

In Eastern philosophy, the soul is composed of eternal energy. The prana (life energy) that separates the living from the dead cannot be destroyed, only changed. The body is created and dissolved, but the soul merely takes on a new shape, or body, each successive lifetime. It is this energy which is our true self. It is in this energy that we transport our experiences and knowledge from one lifetime, as karma, to another life, as the sum of all our lives. Inhabiting a body makes it possible to learn from experiences that can only be achieved in physical form. When we are reborn into another time and body, we are given the opportunity to gain new experiences from a different perspective. The time between incarnations provides knowledge from a non-physical existence.

If body and mind are properly prepared during a lifetime, there is the possibility of using the time after death in a more conscious way. The Tibetan, Egyptian and Christian religions all have special guidebooks about death experiences (Tibetan *Bardo Thödol*, *The Egyptian Book of the Dead* and Christian *Ars Morendi*). These books were written by people so spiritually advanced that they have been able to bring with them knowledge about the various dimensions of human life. The books illustrate the different phases that the soul will experience on its journey to other realms, after leaving the body. They are written as an aid and a guide for the time after death.

The concept of reincarnation is not exclusive to Eastern cultures. Christian doctrine included the idea of reincarnation until the year AD 553 when the Byzantine emperor Justianius condemned it. Before that Origen, one of the most prominent churchmen of the time, wrote, in his opus *De principiis*:

169

The soul has neither beginning nor end . . . Every soul comes to this world strengthened by the victories or weakened by the defeats of its previous life. Its place in this world as a vessel appointed to honour or dishonour is determined by its previous merits or demerits. Its work in this world determines its place in the world which is to follow this.

DEATH, DYING AND IMMORTALITY

Transpersonal experiences in Rebirthing often lead to a questioning of the ageing process, as well as of death and dying. For many the experiences create a new attitude toward death, once the death-urge and deeper layers of fear have been integrated. Death is often seen as a transition rather than a termination and the subject is approached with interest rather than fear. Physical immortality, or at least the prolonging of the lifespan far beyond the normal, is no longer excluded as a possibility.

It is not clear whether this is an inevitable reaction in people who practise some form of breathing exercise, but the search for immortality is found in all the ancient schools. The perception of death as the definite end, has only become widespread through the mechanical world view which has dominated the present century. Most cultures and religions see death as a form of continuity. Many of the world's most famous monuments are examples of this: the Egyptian pyramids and sphinxes, the mausoleum in Halicanassus in ancient Persia, the pre-Colombian pyramids and the temples of Aztec, Olmec and Maya, the great graves of the moguls, the Taj Mahal, the monument of Akbar the Great. They have all been devoted to the dead and the mysteries around death.

In ancient Egypt, the pharaohs were immortal. Death, for them, meant only a transition to heaven, as in the myth of Osiris. The poem of Gilgamesh, one of the most celebrated stories in Babylonian culture (3000 BC), describes immortality. The great prophet Zarathustra (c.1000 – 600 BC) and his disciples, followed this tradition and took a 'drink of immortality' which made them abandon the human condition for closer contact with the god Ahura Mazda. The Greek hymn to Demeter also describes initiation as an attempt to reach immortality. Finally, in the *Rig Veda*, one of the oldest Indian scriptures, there are 120 hymns devoted to the god Soma and the drink of immortality that was drunk in his honour. Soma was said to prolong life, being the guardian against weakness and illness.

> We have drunk Soma
> we have become immortal;
> reached the light,
> we have found the Gods.
> What can ungodliness and meanness
> with the mortal
> do to us now, Oh immortal?
>
> *Rig Veda 8:48, 3*

Mystics and spiritual seekers of all cultures, have not only recognized the soul's immortality, but also tried to develop techniques that would lead to actual physical immortality. They have aimed at moving the soul between the various dimensions without permanently leaving the body. In India, Tibet and China there are many methods, especially breathing exercises, which are meant to lead to physical immortality.

> When the human being has reached divine consciousness, the spiritual power that forms the essence of every breath goes to the crown of the head and stays there. Thereby she is given immortality. But as long as the human being is being ruled by an egoistic, personal life view this invisible life force will be lost.
>
> *Brunton, The Quest of The Overself, 1970*

The various schools of yoga have placed great emphasis on purifying and maintaining the physical body in an ever-youthful condition. The body is seen as the temple for worshipping God and is, therefore, the most reliable tool for mastering death.

> Since liberation can be reached also in this life the body has to be kept for as long as possible and in perfect condition.
>
> *Eliade, From Primitives to Zen, 1969*

171

Goraknath, one of the great figures of Indian history, is said to be one of the founders of Hatha Yoga. It is not clear whether Goraknath was, in fact, an historical person since he appears in a variety of myths. He is regarded as the dominant person behind the yoga theories of physical immortality, linked with the breathing exercises of yoga. A very advanced stage of pranayama aims at teaching how to go through all the levels of consciousness during the pauses between breathing. This is a way to reach a union with the highest consciousness. The pauses can be stretched out until the breathing is virtually stopped. In this state, a yogi can be buried alive for weeks, without the spark of life in the body being lost.

> So long as breath remains in the body there is no death. When the full length of the wind is all confined in the body, nothing being allowed to go out, it is Kevala Kumbhaka.
>
> *Gheranda Samhita, verse 89*

The Tibetan school of yoga has special breathing exercises, 'lung-gom', aimed at healing the body and increasing the lifespan. One exercise, 'che-len', is used to grow longer hair and new teeth, and to extend life. Of the around 21,000 breaths that we normally breathe in a day, approximately 500 are directly life-giving in a special way. Through learning to distinguish them and control the breath, the special life-giving breaths can be increased, thereby extending the growing process and the life span.

Tai I Chin Hua Tsung Chih (The Secret of the Golden Flower), one of the ancient Chinese scriptures, was written on wooden plates in the seventeenth century, after being orally transmitted for a long time. On one of them it is inscribed:

> Master Lu-Stu said, That which exists through itself is called the Way (Tao). Tao has neither name nor shape. It is the one essence, the one primal spirit. Essence and life cannot be seen. They are contained in the light of heaven. The light of heaven cannot be seen.It is contained in the two eyes . . . The great One is the term given to that which has nothing above it . . . Heaven created water

172

through the One. That is the true energy of the great One. If man attains this One he becomes alive; if he loses it he dies. But even if man lives in the energy (vital breath, prana) he does not see the energy, just as fishes live in the water but do not see the water. Man dies when he has no vital breath, just as fishes perish when deprived of water. Therefore the adept have taught people to hold fast to the primal, and to guard the One; it is the circulation of the light and the maintaining of the centre. If one guards this true energy, one can prolong the span of life, and can then apply the method of creating an immortal body by 'melting and mixing'.

Wilhelm, The Secret of The Golden Flower, 1962

In Chinese tradition, the human body is 'made of breaths'. In the beginning of the world there were nine types of breathing which, when mixed, created chaos. When the chaos later was dissolved, the various breaths were separated into the pure and subtle breaths that formed heaven and the impure and forceful breaths that became earth. The first great god evolved from knots in the breaths. Since the human being is created of the impure breaths, he or she has to completely replace the breath with the pure form. This is the goal of 'embryonic respiration'. It is aimed at prolonging life and 'as a material immortality of the body itself' (Maspero, 1937). This is one of many breathing exercises designed to slow down or stop the breathing. One prescription states, for instance, that the aim is to hold the breath for the time required to take 1,000 breaths. This will lead to physical immortality.

Here again, it is essential to point out that all the ancient techniques aimed at physical immortality were designed for use by people who devote their entire lives to spiritual pursuit. It is essential that practitioners of these techniques should have acquired a profound understanding of altered states of consciousness and the physical limitations of their bodies. They also need to be fully aware of the life-threatening risks they are taking in the search for immortality. If these prerequisites are not fully understood and/or treated with the appropriate respect by novice spiritual seekers, they can be very

173

dangerous paths to pursue. I therefore strongly warn against any attempts at the above mentioned techniques, without proper guidance and a full understanding of all the risks involved.

THE NEW AGE

Since Rebirthing is often described as a 'New Age Therapy', we shall conclude this section on the spirituality of breathing by looking at the meaning of the term 'new age'. The idea that we are now at the beginning of a new age, or new era, has its roots in the Eastern world view. According to the Indian tradition, we live in the darkest of all ages. It sees time as cyclical and divided into gigantic kalpas (time periods). A kalpa is as long as a day and a night in the life of Brahman (the divine creator).

> A kalpa is the time needed for an angel to come down from heaven, once a year, to sweep her wing over the top of a high mountain and thus wear it down to the ground.
>
> *Indian sutra*

A kalpa is divided into mahayugas (great eras), reflecting the spiritual level of mankind. They reach from the darkest time, where people live completely in the material world, to the brightest, where people reach the highest level of consciousness and spiritual development. (The origin of the ancient knowledge as well as the gods and goddesses of mythology is said to come from these enlightened eras.) The present time, Kali yuga, can also be divided into shorter periods. We are, in present time, reaching the final phase of the dark era. The 'New Age' reflects the transition to a new era with a higher level of consciousness.

These changes are also described in terms of the yin-yang movements which influence all phenomena in the universe. Once an expanding movement reaches a climax, it changes over to its opposite contraction. The movement tends to accelerate, getting faster and faster. This is comparable to today's society in which changes are made at an increasing speed. What before took hundreds of years to alter can now change in a few years. We can communicate with all parts of the world instantaneously. News of events can create shock waves that sweep over the continents several times a day. There are no longer vast regions of the world excluded from influence by the rest. We have all become united, whether we like it or not.

For a long time the feminine yin force has been more or less passive in society for various reasons. The Western world, in particular, has been highly oriented towards the male yang influence, with its dominance of rational thinking, technical solutions, restless activity, aggression, etc. Many people today live their lives without a special focus or overall principle which might instruct them how to live in harmony with nature. All of this leads, according to the Hindu world view, to disturbance and destruction, the signs of the final phase of Kali Yuga. At the end of each era, the god Shiva and his wife Mahakali, are said to unleash a period of destruction of the prevailing order, so as to make room for a new and better world.

Everyone would probably agree that we live in a world in crisis. Reports about destruction of the environment, AIDS and other illnesses, war, violence and moral decay seem to have an increasing part in everyday life. At the same time positive changes have started to take place and there is a growing consciousness that something must be done to save the planet for future generations.

The Chinese sign for crisis consists of the sign for danger in combination with the sign for development and the possibility of change. A crisis is not just a dangerous situation but also an opportunity to change. The change that our planet most needs, though, has to come from within individuals. Not until people can feel compassion and love for themselves can they fully feel love and compassion for others. Not until people have learnt to care about themselves can they really care for others. Only when we have learnt to love and understand ourselves, and got rid of our anger and fear, can we let our consciousness move from a focus on personal needs to an awareness of the needs of others. Not until then can a permanent change take place. Then we will have no more internal need for destruction and conflict, based on our negative thoughts. Then we can really start changing negative trends and develop a global consciousness.

After the creative forces retreat, they return. In human affairs those of like mind and character join harmoniously together in new undertakings. This mirrors the movement of the Tao. There is movement but not brought about by force. The movement is natural, arising spontaneously. For this reason the transformation of the old becomes easy. The old is discarded and the new introduced. Both measures accord with the time; therefore no harm results.

I Ching

Resource Addresses

Argentina

Jorge Brusca
Beruti 2446
5th floor A
Buenos Aires 1117
Tel: 0541 83 69 11

Australia

Christina Artemis
PO Box 488
Mudgeeraba Qld 4213
Tel: 075 305 058

Breath Connection
PO Box 6054
191 Magellan Street
South Lismore
NSW 2480
Tel: 066 220 155

Kim Byatt
323 Fitzgerald Street
North Perth WA 6006
Tel: 09 328 9614

Austria

Atem-Kultur Zentrum
Gabi Durkowitsch
Hermanngasse 30
1070 Wien
Tel: 0222 52 64 750

ATMAN–Österreichischer Verein
    für Rebirthing und spirituelles
    Wachstum
Dr Willfried Ehrmann
Eichendorffgasse 8/17
1190 Wien
Tel: 0222 369 23 63

Synergie-Zentrum
Alter platz 4
9020 Klagenfurt
Tel: 0463 26 11 23

Heimo Grimm
Anzengruberstrasse 40
9020 Klagenfurt
Tel: 0463 26 11 23

Belgium

Genevieve Migeal
140 Avenue du Diamant
1040 Breuxelles
Tel: 02 736 6456

Brazil

Aldo de Andrade E. Sousa Ficao
av Princesa Isabel no 334-BL-2
    Apt 705
Rio de Janeiro R J 22011
Tel: 021 542 2909

Virginia de Souza Jahara
Ava Raimundo Correra 43
    Apt 302
Copacabana
Rio de Janeiro
Tel: 021 742 2568

Bulgaria

Ilia Wassilev
1799 Sofia
Mladost 2.BL.219.VH.A. APP.12
Tel: 02 773 537

Zwetomir Manov
Veliko Tarnovo
Ul. 'Sedmi Uli' 11

Verka Petrova
5300 Gabrovo
Ul. 'Evtim Dabev' 2.VH.B.
Tel: 066 263 65

Canada

Claude Charlebois
1565 Arsenault
Ste-Rose
Laval
QU H7L 4J8
Tel: 0514 628 0574

Lynne Jenkins
485 Huron Street #403
Toronto
ONT M5R 2R5
Tel: 416 928 2734

Gita Kandiah
Suite 304
8830–85 Street
Edmonton
Alberta T6C 3CS
Tel: 0403 466 1890

George Taillon
2400 Montée-Gagnon
Montreal
Quebec J7E 4H5
Tel: 0514 437 4173

Colombia

Fanny De Carrillo
Carrera 18 #63-64
Bogota
Tel: 02 249 0215/01 248 0215

Commonwealth of Independent States (formerly Soviet Union)

International Association for Free
  Breathing
142092 Troitsk V-3-124
Moscow
Fax: 7095 420 1042

Dr Sergei Gorsky
Founder and coordinator
Moscow
Tel: 7096 601 6528

Andrei and Svetlana Shakhov
Secretaires and trainers
Moscow
Tel: 7095 208 5491

Galina Shibaeva
Translator and trainer
Moscow
Tel: 7095 302 3272

Dr Michael Molokanov
Trainer and research coordinator
Moscow
Tel: 7095 905 6479

Sergei Strekalov
Trainer
St Petersburg
Tel: 7812 150 3792

Vladimir Kozlov
Trainer and author
Yaroslavl
Tel: 7085 222 2594

Denmark

Danish Society for Rebirthing
c/o Finn Andersen
Lodager 13
2620 Albertslund
Copenhagen
Tel: 426 45604

France

Laurence Lundell
155 Rue de l'Université
Paris 75007
Tel: 01 45 55 10 46

Germany

Sarito Griebl
Parzivalstrasse 23
8000 München 40
Tel: 089 364 370

Barbara Jansohn-Franz
Gartenfeldplatz 10
6500 Mainz
Tel: 061 31 67 43 82

Dr Rudiger Stellberg
Oststrasse 152 TAO
40210 Düsseldorf
Tel: 0211 36 95 11

Pfad-Zentrum
Stresemannstrasse 21
1 Berlin 61
Tel: 030 25 13 180

Ireland

Joe Dooley
11 Ballsbridge Avenue
Ballsbridge
Dublin 04
Tel: 01 660 9925

Italy

Robin Lawley
The Creative Development
    Foundation
Vale S. Ignazio di Loyla 9
Parco delle Rose
801 31 Napoli
Tel: 081 587 2252

Israel

Gilad Schafman
27 Zlatopolsky St
Tel-Aviv 63475
Tel: 03 524 3102

Mexico

Tari Benvenuti
AP Postal 43
48970 Cihuatlan JAL
Tel: 0333 700 50

Gidi and Nati Bar-Shalom
New Age Book Store
4 Habima Square
Tel-Aviv
Tel: W 9723 562 4989
    H 9723 528 8006

New Zealand

'Further Dimensions'
Holistic Health Nurse Consultants
Lorraine Anderson/Barbara
    Maunder
3 Parkview Place
Pakuranga
Auckland
Tel: 09 576 6762

Ada Alkapuri Mirsky
27 Jorden Street
Ramat-Gan 52281
Tel: 9723 741 558

Stephanie Rosenbaum
16-A Herman Cohen
Tel-Aviv 64385
Tel: 9723 524 5056

New Zealand Association of
    Rebirthers
Liz Hart
53 Kiwitea Street
Sandringham
Auckland
Tel: 09 629 3375

Rafael Tishby
4 Metula Street
Ramat-Gan

Open Circle of Rebirth
Alison Gilmore
28 Smith Street
Christchurch

Poland

Holistyczna Akademia Wzrostu
'Lajwanti i Laxami'
Jolanta Laxami-Wdowiak
Solikowskiego 1A/5
80-393 Gdansk Oliwa
Tel: 058 56 10 67

Polskie Centrum Rebirthingu
Ekologieczny Osrodek
  Szkoleniowo-Treningowy Metod
  Rozwoju
Potencjalu Ludzkiego
Silna Nowa 24
66-330 Pszczew
Woj. Gorzowskie

Republic of South Africa

Janet Crouse
29 Pentlands Road
Blairgowrie 2194
Tel: 011 782 6547

Hilde Light
PO Box 2913
Cresta 2118
Tel: 011 477 7004

Spain

Bam, Bam, Bhole Baba and
  Rebirthing Centre
Vrindavana Mavi Carreres
Apartado de Correos 251
46160 Liria
Valencia
Tel: 6 278 30 17

Montserrat Mestre Gallinat and
  Anand Crisostomo
Tamarit 134, 5°2a
08015 Barcelona
Tel: 424 4506
Fax: 423 8669

Rosa M. Livia Vazsuez Garcia
c) Sant Eduard 22A 2*1*
Sant Cugat
Barcelona 08190
Tel: 675 0958

Mikaela Marin Noguera
Enrique Granados 114 401a
08008 Barcelona
Tel: 093 415 2437

Sweden

Föreningen för Frigörande
  Andning
Sågstuvägen 16
141 49 Huddinge
Tel: 08 779 30 01

Wäxthuset
Fjäll 6908
760 40 Väddö
Tel: 0175 314 85/316 17

Switzerland

Anita Rüegsegger
16 Grange-Lévrier
1220 Genève
Tel: 022 797 14 27

École d'Évolution Personelle et
  Spirituelle
Joy Manné
150 Ch. Crêt-de-Plan
1093 La Conversion s/Lutry
Tel: 021 791 30 84 (8h00 9h00)

United States

Inspiration University
(Leonard Orr)
PO Box 5320
Chico CA 96927
Tel: 916 893 8643

United Kingdom

British Rebirth Society
c/o Montgomery
5 Manor Road
Catcott
Bridgewater
Somerset TA7 9HT
Tel: 0278 722 536

Sheffield Birth and Healing Centre
71 Crescent Road
Nether Edge
Sheffield S7 1HN
Tel: 0742 509 759

Holistic Rebirthing Institute
Lee Preisler
Dove Villa
99 Radford Road
Leamington Spa
Warks CV31 1JZ
Tel: 0926 882 494

Loving Relationship Training
Diane Roberts and Ben Renshaw
4 Lower Belgrave Street
London SW1
Tel: 071 730 5349

Vivation
Hilary Newman
79a Acre Lane
London SW2 5TN
Tel: 071 733 9774

Rebirth Associates of Los Angeles
Dr. Eve Jones, PhD
140 S. Norton Avenue
Los Angeles CA 90004
Tel: 213 461 5774

Vivation (Publishing) Co
Phil Laut
PO Box 8269
Cincinnati OH 45208
Tel: 1 800 597 1923/
  513 321 4405

Venezuela

Sanchez B. Magaly
calle Chimborazo ata El Fortin
  Chvao
Caracas
Tel: 920 683

West Indies

Kari Willcox
PO Box 164
Westerhall Fort Jeudy
Grenada

Bibliography

Albery, Nicolas: *How to Feel Reborn?* Regeneration Press, London 1985.

Avedon, John F.: *In Exile from the Land of Snows*, Michael Joseph Ltd, London, 1984.

Benson, Herbert and Klipper, Miriam Z.: *The Relaxation Response*, Fount Paperbacks, London, 1977.

Berendt, Joachim-Ernst: *Nada Brahma The World is Sound*, Destiny Books, Rochester, Vermont, 1987.

Bergland, Richard: *The Fabric of Mind*, Penguin Books, Harmondsworth, 1985.

Bhattacharya, D.N.: *Kriya Yoga*, P.K. Mukherjee, Calcuttta, 1980.

Bjerre, J.: *Kalahari*, Michael Joseph, London, 1960.

Brunton, Paul: *The Quest of the Overself*, Rider, London, 1970.

Burmeister, Mary: *Jin Shin Jyutsu is*, Jin Shin Jyutsu Inc, Arizona, 1980.

Burnett Taylor, Edward: *Religion in Primitive Culture*, Harper Torchbook, New York, 1958.

Byrom, T: *The Dhammapada – The Sayings of the Buddha*, Vintage, New York, 1976.

Calder, Nigel: *Einstein's Universe*, Penguin, Harmondsworth, 1990.

Capra, Fritjof: *The Tao of Physics*, 3rd ed., Fontana, London, 1992.

Capra, Fritjof: *The Turning Point*, Fontana, London, 1985.

Capra, Fritjof: *Uncommon Wisdom*, Fontana, London, 1989.

Chew, Geoffrey: 'Bootstrap: A Scientific Idea?', *Science* Vol 161, 23 May, 1968.

Clifford, Terry: *Tibetan Buddhist Medicine and Psychiatry – The Diamond Healing*, Samuel Wieser Inc, York Beach, Maine, 1984.

Corsini, Raymond: *Handbook of Innovative Psychotherapies*, John Wiley & Sons, New York, 1981.

Crookall, Robert: *Psychic Breathing, Cosmic Vitality From the Air*, Newcastle Publishing Co. Inc, California, 1985.

David-Neel, Alexandra: *Magic and Mystery in Tibet*, Mandala, London, 1984.

Davies, Paul: *The Cosmic Blueprint*, Unwin Hyman, London, 1989.

Davies, P.C.W., and Brown, J: *Superstrings A Theory of Everything?*, Cambridge University Press, Cambridge, 1988.

de Chardin, Teilhard: *The Phenomenon of Man*, Harper Torchbooks, New York, 1965.

de Dacia, Petrus: *Om den Saliga Jungfrun Kristina av Stommeln*, Bonniers, Stockholm, 1965.

Dick-Read, G.: *Childbirth without Fear*, Harper & Row, New York, 1968.

Doore, Gary: *Shaman's Path*, Shambala, Boston, 1988.

Doresse, Jean: *The Secret Books of the Egyptian Gnostics*, Inner Tradition Ltd, New York, USA, 1986.

Dudley, G.A.: *Dreams, Their Mystery Revealed*, Aquarian, Wellingborough, 1979.

Dyer, Wayne: *The Sky's the Limit*, Granada, New York, 1980.

Easwaran, Eknath: *Introduction to Dhammapada*, Arkana, London, 1986.

Eliade, Mircea: *A History of Religious Ideas*, Vol 1, Chicago Press, Chicago, 1978.

Eliade, Mircea: *A History of Religious Ideas*, Vol 2, Chicago Press, Chicago, 1982.

Eliade, Mircea: *From Primitives to Zen*, The Chaucer Press Ltd, Suffolk England, 1967.

Eliade, Mircea: *Yoga and Immortality*, Princeton Press, Princeton, 1969.

Fedor-Freybergh, Peter, and Vogel, Vanessa: *Prenatal and Perinatal Psychology and Medicine*, Parthenon Publishing, Carnforth, Lancs., 1988.

Ferguson, Marilyn: *The Aquarian Conspiracy*, Granada, London, 1984.

Ferguson, Marilyn: *The Brain Revolution*, Bantam, New York, 1973.

Field, Reshad: *Here to Heal*, Element Books, Dorset, 1985.

Funderburk, James: *Science studies Yoga*, Himalayan International Institute of Yoga Science and Philosophy, USA, 1977.

Gawain, Shakti: *Creative Visualization*, New World Library, San Rafael, CA, 1985.

Goodard, Dwight: *Bhuddhist Bible*, Harrap, London, 1957.

Govinda, Lama Anagarika: *Foundations of Tibetan Mysticism*, Rider & Co, London, 1960.

Grenier, Jean: *Tao, Natur och Kultur*, Stockholm, 1980.

Gribbin, John: *In Search of the Big Bang*, Corgi, London, 1987.

Gribbin, John: *The Search for Schrödingers Cat*, Corgi, London, 1985.

Grof, Stanislav: *Ancient Wisdom and Modern Science*, State University of New York Press, Albany, 1984.

Grof, Stanislav: *Beyond the Brain*, State University of New York Press, New York, 1985.

Grof, Stanislav: *The Adventure of Self-Discovery*, State University of New York Press, Albany, 1988.

Grof, Stanislav: *The Human Encounter with Death*, E.P. Dutton, New York, 1977.

Grof, Stanislav: *Realms of the Human Unconscious*, Viking Press, New York, 1975.

Grof, Stanislav, and Grof, Christina: *The Stormy Search for the Self*, Mandala, London, 1991.

Grof, Stanislav, and Grof, Christina: *Spiritual Emergency*, Jeremy P. Tarcher, Los Angeles, 1989.

Hay, Louise L: *You Can Heal Your Life*, Hay House, California, 1987.

Hayward, Jeremy W: *Shifting Worlds Changing Minds*, New Science Library, London, 1987.

Herman, Sonya: *The Miracle of Breath, Thought and Love*, Assertive Training Institute, California, 1980.

Hoff, Benjamin: *The Tao of Pooh*, Mandarin, London, 1990.

Inglis, Brian: *Natural Medicine*, Fontana, London, 1981.

Jampolsky, Gerald: *Love is Letting go of Fear*, Celestial Arts, California, 1979.

Janov, Arthur: *The Anatomy of Mental Illness*, Berkley Medallion Books, New York, 1971.

Janov, Arthur: *Imprints*, Coward & McCann, New York, 1983.

Janov, Arthur: *The Primal Revolution*, The Garnstone Press Ltd, London, 1972.

Janov, Arthur and Holden, Michael: *Primal Man*, Thomas Y Gowrell Co, New York, 1975.

Janov, Arthur: *The Primal Scream*, Abacus, 1970 (new edition 1992, *New Primal Scream*).

Johari, Harish: *Chakras, Energy Centers of Transformation*, Destiny Books, Vermont, 1987.

Jones, Eve: *An Introduction to Rebirthing for Health Professionals*, Life Unlimited Books, Los Angeles, CA, 1982.

Jung, Carl Gustav: *Memories, Dreams, Reflections*, Flamingo, London, 1983.

Kapleau, Philip: *The Three Pillars of Zen*, Beacon Press, Boston, 1967.

Kelder, Peter: *Tibetan Secrets of Youth and Vitality*, Aquarian, Wellingborough, 1988.

Leboyer, Frederick: *Birth Without Violence*, Penguin, 1990.

Leonard, Jim, and Laut, Phil: *Rebirthing - the Science of Enjoying All of Your Life*, Trinity Publications, California, 1983.

Magarian, Gregory J.: *Hyperventilation Syndromes*, The Williams and Wilkins Co, USA, 1982.

Main, Michael: *Kalahari*, Southern Book Publishers, Johannesburg, 1987.

Mandel, Bob: *Open Heart Therapy*, Celestial Arts, California, 1984.

Mandel, Bob, and Ray, Sondra: *Birth and Relationships*, Celestial Arts, California, 1987.

Mascaro, Juan (trans): *The Bhagavad Gita*, Penguin Classics, Middlesex, 1962.

Mascaro, Juan (trans): *The Upanishads*, Penguin, Harmondsworth, 1965.

Maspero, Henri: 'Les proceds de "nourrir le principe vital" dans la religion taoiste ancienne', *JA*, 1937.

Melzack, Ronald: *The Puzzle of Pain*, Basic Books, New York, 1973.

Mumford, John: *Psychosomatic Yoga*, Samuel Weiser Inc, New York, 1979.

Orr, Leonard, and Ray, Sondra: *Rebirthing in the New Age*, Celestial Arts, California, 1977.

Orr, Leonard: *Breath Awareness*, Inspiration University, California, 1986.

Orr, Leonard: *The Common Sense of Physical Immortality*, Inspiration University, California, 1987.

Orr, Leonard: *Physical Immortality, The science of everlasting life*, Inspiration University, California, 1980.

Paramahansa Yogananda: *Autobiography of a Yogi*, Self Realization Fellowship, Los Angeles, 1977.

Pribram, Karl H.: *Languages of the Brain*, Prentice Hall, New Jersey, 1971.

Ray, Sondra: *Celebration of Breath*, Celestial Arts, California, 1983.

Ray, Sondra: *I Deserve Love*, Celestial Arts, Berkeley Ca, 1976.

Ray, Sondra: *Ideal Birth*, Celestial Arts, Berkeley Ca, 1985.

Ray, Sondra: *Loving Relationships*, Celestial Arts, Berkeley Ca, 1980.

Reich, Wilhelm: *Character Analysis*, Vision Press Ltd, London, 1973.

Reich, Wilhelm: *The Function of the Orgasm*, Orgone Institute Press, New York, 1942.

Rosenthal, Robert, and Jacobson, Leora: *Teachers, Expectancies, Determinant of Pupils IQ Gains*, Psychological Reports 19 (1).

Russell, Peter: *Awakening Earth*, Arkana, 1991.

Russell, Peter: *The Brain Book - Know Your Own Mind and How to Use It*, Routledge, 1990.

Russell, William R.: *Explaining the Brain*, Oxford University Press, Oxford, 1975.

Sanella, Leo: *Kundalini, Psychosis or Transcendence?*, H.S. Dakin Co, San Francisco, 1977.

Sheldrake, Rupert: *A New Science of Life*, Paladin, London, 1985.

Shyam, Radhe: *I am Harmony*, The Spanish Creek Press, Crestone CO, USA, 1989.

Sing, Pancham: *The Hatha Yoga Pradipika*, Oriental Books, New Delhi, 1975.

Sisson, Colin P.: *Rebirthing Made Easy*, Hayhouse, California, 1987.

Sisson, Colin P.: *Breath of Life*, Total Press Ltd, Auckland, 1989.

Srisa Chandra Vasu, and Rai, Bahadur: *The Gheranda Samhita*, Oriental Books Reprint Co, New Delhi, 1975.

Srisa Chandra Vasu, and Rai, Bahadur: *Siva Samhita*, Oriental Books Reprint Co, New Delhi, 1975.

Treadway, Scott, and Treadway, Linda: *Ayurveda and Immortality*, Celestial Arts, Berkley, California, 1986.

Verny, Thomas: *The Secret Life of the Unborn Child*, Delta, USA, 1988.

Versluis, Arthur: *The Egyptian Mysteries*, Arkana, London, 1988.

van Lysbeth, Andre: *Pranayama, the Yoga of Breathing*, Unwin Hyman, London, 1979.

Watson, Lyall: *Supernature II*, Hodder and Stoughton, London, 1987.

Wentz, Evan: *The Tibetan Book of the Dead*, Oxford University Press, Oxford, 1980.

Wilber, Ken: *Quantum Questions, Mystical Writings of the World's Greatest Physicists*, New Science Library, London, 1985.

Wilhelm, Richard: *The Secret of the Golden Flower*, Harvest/HBJ Books, New York, 1962.

Woodroffe, John: *The Serpent Power*, Ganesh & Co, Madras, 1972.

von Glasenapp, Helmuth: *Indisk Filosofi*, Studentlitteratur, Lund, 1980.

Yogi Ramanchara: *The Hindu-Yogi Science of Breath*, L.N. Fowler & Co. London.

Zaehner, R.C. (trans): *Bhagavad Ghita*, J.M. Dent & Sons Ltd, London, 1966.

Zang, Ming wu Sun Xingyuan: *Chinese Qigong Therapy*, Shandong Science and Technology Press, Jinan, China, 1985.

Zi, Nancy: *The Art of Breathing*, Bantam Books, New York, 1986.

Zukav, Gary: *The Dancing Wu Li Masters*, Rider, 1991.

Index

acupuncture 15, 78
affirmation techniques 88, 125-7, 128-9, 160
ageing process 87, 170
alkalosis 66
altitudes, high, effects of 18
analysis, mutual 118
anesthesia, positive feedback during 79
anger 121, 127
Aqua Energetics 132
attitude, changed 103, 118-24, 127-8
aura 73
autosuggestion 79
ayurvedic medicine 77-8

behaviour *see* attitude, changed
birth trauma 23, 50, 80-1, 103-10, 112
birth-death cycle ix, 51
blood-brain barrier 71-2
body movements 43-4
body sensations 43, 44-5
Body-Harmony 132
brain 66-72, 82-3, 93
  degeneration 86-7
  gate mechanisms 31, 94, 97-9, 100, 102
  integration of two sides 18, 68
  potential 16
  processing in 95-6, 97, 121-2
breathing
  alternated nasal 54

cultural semantics 144-5
effect on brain 71-2
of energy ix, 30, 53, 54, 173
inner 60, 73, 148
in modern therapies 131-5
physiology of 59-67
in Rebirthing 28, 31-3, 53-4
spontaneous 44
types 34-6, 38-41
see also conscious breathing; conscious connected breathing
breathing sessions 25-8
British Rebirth Society 2

cancer 79, 84-6
cerebrospinal system 49
chakras 2, 49, 73-5, 134
Chi Gong 37-8
childbirth 79-81
Chinese tradition 37-41, 172-3
Chinese traditional medicine 78
circulation 19-20
claustrophobia 112
cleansing 19-20, 93, 151
COEX system 114-15
collective consciousness theories 168
collective unconscious 164-5
colour therapy 78-9
conscious breathing 19, 23, 102, 168
  applications 7-8, 145-50
  first-time experience 5-6
  and psychosomatic illness 84
  spiritual purpose 146

189